Revised Edition

HOUSE RABBIT HANDBOOK

How to Live with an Urban Rabbit

By Marinell Harriman
Drollery Press

To Herman, who opened the door;
To Phoebe, who has kept it open.

Drollery Press, Alameda
in association with David Lewis
and Joyce Haven

Photographs by the author.
Additional photographs by Amy Shapiro,
Tania Harriman, and as noted.

Production: Robert Harriman
Digital prep: ProPer Publishing
Printing: Kingsport Press

Library of Congress Cataloging-in-Publication Data
Harriman, Marinell, 1941–
    House rabbit handbook : how to live with an urban rabbit / by
Marinell Harriman. -- Rev. ed.
               p.   cm.
    Includes index.
    ISBN 0-940920-07-7 : $8.95
    1. Rabbits. 2. Rabbits--Anecdotes. I. Title. II. Title: Urban
rabbit.
SF453.H37   1991   91-10009
636'.9322--dc20   CIP

Drollery Press
1524 Benton Street
Alameda, California 94501

CONTENTS

PHOTO: BOB HARRIMAN

Preface

HOUSE RABBITS ARE HERE to stay. It wasn't just a passing fad. People of all ages have become enlightened to the joys of having a rabbit in the house. If you are open-minded to alternative house rules and enjoy watching and learning from other species, a rabbit as a housepet can be a pleasure you never before imagined. My intention is to help you find that pleasure.

This book is for pet owners only. I offer no recipes for rabbit stew, no instructions for pelting and selling rabbit fur and no guidelines of any kind for commercial rabbit raising. Furthermore, I hope to convince you that your pet rabbit should not live in an outdoor hutch, but rather in your house where potential for the human-animal bond can be optimized. Even if you're away at work all day, this roommate is with you when you brush your teeth at night and when your alarm goes off in the morning. Could a rabbit caged outdoors receive as much attention as a by-product of your daily routine? How much time can you spend standing at a rabbit hutch in the backyard? Indoors, we are dealing with different animals, and the personalities that emerge in a human world are as individual as their human housemates.

At the printing of the first edition, I was hoping to find a thousand people with an interest in rabbits as housepets. The next three years produced a number that was over twenty-five times my expectation and resulted in the formation of the House Rabbit Society. This non-profit organization networks rabbit friends across the country and also rescues and fosters homeless rabbits. Volunteer fosterers have had the opportunity to live with and learn from hundreds of new rabbits each year in various geographic areas.

Behavior information in this edition comes from my own rabbit foster-home, from the foster homes of Amy Shapiro, Susan Stark, Margo DeMello and Holly O'Meara. It also comes from a broad base of individual rabbit homes.

ACKNOWLEDGMENTS

We thank the following participants for sharing experiences and photographs:

Helen Lau, Franklin Chow, Dan Donahue, Beth Woolbright, Cheryl O'Connell, Ken O'Connell, Rachael Millan, Amy Berg, Hugh Douglas, Kingstone Shih, Michelle Okino, Mary Lee Nafus, Steve Nafus, Joyce Haven, Lynda Allston, Bill Webb, Mary Alice Mita, Ron Mita, Paul Knapp, Kathy Kifer, Don Latarski, Jack Rosenberger, Betty Tsubamoto, Carolyn Long, Terry Valerio, Jesus Valerio, Judy Morin, Kim Stiewig, Melanie Cresci, Kay Leiker, Eleanor Grams, Mark Lichtenfeld, Bill Yaden, Elizabeth TeSelle, Kari Gilje, Patty Hastreiter, Charlie Esple, Carol-Molly Prier, Melinda Bascone, and Richard Dow.

We are extremely grateful to Drs. Marliss Geissler, Carolynn Harvey and Richard Evans for sharing their vast knowledge in the area of rabbit health; for extending our rabbits' lives, both in length and quality; and for so generously giving time in solving both general and specific problems.

Toward A New Definition

THEY COME IN ALL SIZES, shapes and personalities. In fact, a house rabbit is the result not of a breeding program, but rather, an individual program of time, patience, shared living space, and adjusted lifestyles.

Biologists can tell you what rabbits are made of and what their organs are like. Stock raisers can talk about the prices of flesh and fur. Show judges can describe physical standards of particular breeds. But who can describe the characteristics of *house* rabbits better than those who live with them and love them? There are many of us now—rabbit owners across the country, who are eager to share experiences, dispel the myths, and tell the world of our discoveries.

Our house-rabbit family-members, young and old, large and small, have exposed the errors in the way that rabbits have been defined. For too long rabbits have been mislabeled, misunderstood and underrated as pets. Only through the intimate environment of loving homes can their true nature, needs, behaviors and abilities be revealed to humans.

PHOTO OPPOSITE: HELEN LAU. ABOVE: BOB HARRIMAN

THE PUZZLE OVER RABBIT SENSE

Of course you know what rabbits look like, but what do you know of their "minds"? Housed in small heads, their brains have been considered lacking in mental abilities. Yet anyone who knows them as housepets has seen them perform beyond their supposed capacities. Perhaps, like other animals when given some freedom, they are able to fully develop their underrated brains and show what they can do.

Personalities and intelligence do vary with individuals, but certain characteristics are present in all house rabbits. All are capable of giving and receiving affection, each in his own way. Some lick; some rub noses; some may sit on your lap; others prefer to sit beside you. They all can learn to enjoy your company.

GOOD OL' BOYS (AND GIRLS)

Enthusiasm from the owners of older rabbits shows a pattern in house rabbit develop-ment. They all seem to get better with time (or perhaps it's our own understanding that gets better with time). Most will go through an exasperating adolescence before blossoming into model housepets with reliable habits. They become easier to manage and can even be housetrained when well past their prime. Often they don't reach their maximum poten-tial for a relationship with humans until after the first year. Unfortunately, too many are never given the opportunity to prove it.

You can call it intelligence, instinct, condi-tioning or whatever, but they can learn to manipulate humans. That beguiling posture of inno-cence after a misdeed is familiar to anyone who lives with a house rabbit. They can also learn less intuitive things like how to push with their feet on doors that open outward and to pull with their teeth on doors that open inward. They can learn routines. They can learn to use a litterbox, to come when they're called, and to sit up and beg for a treat. They can quickly memorize where all the snacks are kept, and they're smart enough to be sneaky.

A veiled mystery: Waiting to be discovered (left) is a playful creature who can change your life forever.
What's in a box? That's for inquisitive minds (right) to find out.

BOUNDLESS CURIOSITY

All rabbits are inquisitive, and all are capa-ble of mischief—leave your album covers or notebooks on the floor and try to retrieve them an hour later. And like small human children, house rabbits know when you're on the phone!

"All rabbits are inquisitive, and all are capable of mischief."

PHOTO: AMY SHAPIRO

"Many play games of their own invention."

They often like to play—with toys, with other pets or with their human companions. Many play games of their own invention. Some can be stimulated to play by your silly talk or laughter and will respond with their own style of silliness (like a leap straight up with a 180° turn in mid-air). Like dogs and cats, rabbits are responsive to your moods and tone of voice.

TIMID AND BOLD

Rabbits are perceived as timid because of their sensitivity and quick response to sharp noises and sudden movements. In other words, they're easily startled—as they should be. Few species on earth have as many predators (including humans) after their hides. Yet some will stand their ground and even attack. They may be docile, but many are courageous.

Domestic rabbits are natural burrowers, not tree climbers. In your house their territory

Rabbit Watching

By Beth Woolbright

ONE OF THE BY-PRODUCTS, I've decided, of sharing one's home with a free-running rabbit is that this long-eared roommate has often proved to be a mighty large distraction. For one thing, bunnies are so innately cute that they are hard to ignore, but that is especially so when the little critters go around doing those things in life that just come naturally.

For instance, there is something very sweet about the way a rabbit washes his face. And who among us can look upon a rabbit that has "kicked back" on the hearth—slowly slipping into bunny sleep—and yet be able to suppress laughter at the enormous dimensions of a rabbit's hind feet?

Whether it's observing bunny disappear into a waste basket only to reappear seconds later with a banana-peel snack or seeing her stand up on hind legs to get a taller view of the world, house rabbits are a pleasure to watch as they do their thing. ⤴

PHOTO: AMY SHAPIRO. SIDEBAR: MARINELL HARRIMAN

is the floor, not counter tops and dressers. Think of this when Thumper acts agitated over being held in your arms five feet off the ground. Also, you can think of this if you're a naturalist who feels guilty over using a cage at all. A cage has a different meaning when used only as a resting burrow and not as a prison.

At times several of your bunny's natural inclinations may conflict. When Thumper's compulsive curiosity overpowers his aversion to heights, you might find him awkwardly bumping around on your table. Don't expect the grace of a high-climbing cat.

COMMON RABBIT HABITS

The notion that rabbit are nocturnal is dangerous when maintained by people whose rabbits are loose in the yard at night. Rabbits are in fact crepuscular—meaning, most active at dawn and twilight. In our rabbit foster-home, we enjoy their early evening antics, but we bring our rabbits inside when the sun goes down and the predators come out.

Rabbits living in a human house have a "down time" during the day. For this long period of lethargy, most house rabbits will seek the solitude of a cage or find a place to nap under a bed or perhaps a table. Sometimes sleep will overtake them, and they flop wherever they happen to be.

Down-time does have advantages. It builds itself into a human schedule so well that the time you spend away from your rabbit is the time he will normally nap. I've been given so many odd answers to the question, "What is your rabbit's most active time of day?" that I've come to realize that house rabbits have a marvelous way of fitting into a human schedule and will respond to *any* consistent routine.

Ready for action: Bright and alert (left) is one rabbit mode. Ready for a nap: Drowsy and lazy is another mode (right). Both say Rabbit.

PHOTO ABOVE LEFT: AMY SHAPIRO. ABOVE RIGHT: MARINELL HARRIMAN

HOUSE RABBITS SPEAK OUT

The big yawn: Contentment and a sense of well-being are evident to even the most illiterate in rabbit language.

W E'VE ADDED TO OUR VOCABULARY of rabbit language since the first edition of *House Rabbit Handbook.* Our teachers (the foster rabbits) come to us from many different backgrounds. Because rabbits who live in House Rabbit Society foster homes are neutered, volunteers can maintain them in groups without the specter of overpopulation and ensuing disease. This provides opportunity for learning how they communicate with each other and how they apply their language to humans. Rabbits bring with them their native outdoor language and natural responses when they move into their new territory—the house.

Rabbits, living with different people, may develop different "dialects." House rabbit language, therefore, is not as completely defined by observers of wild rabbits as by the person who lives with the rabbit. Just as in our own language we have homonyms (the same words with different meanings) so do rabbits. The important thing to bear in mind is context.

LOCAL LANGUAGE

One of the first signs of contentment is "tooth purring," while being talked to or petted. This is a series of fast but light vibrations of the teeth, which also causes the whiskers to quiver happily. This is not to be confused with a condition of discomfort, expressed in teeth crunching which is usually a louder, slower, single grind (sometimes along with protruding eyes). Again, context will help you distinguish a happy grind from a painful grind .

There is no mistaking the affection intended by licking. Another show of affection, often overlooked by many people, is nose rubbing. Many house rabbits like to nuzzle nose-to-nose with their friends. Nudging your ankle or tugging on your pantleg means, Notice me. Nipping, on the other hand, means, Move over.

BODY STATEMENTS

More subtle than that of a dog or cat, rabbit language can be "read" once the owners are sensitized especially to body positions. Much

PHOTO: WRENN DABNEY REED

"Much is told by the position of the ears, tail and feet."

is told by the position of the ears, tail and feet. The ears may be lazy or alert. They can also be tightly pulled back, giving a menacing look.

FEET FIRST

Feet do a lot of the talking. In comfort they stretch straight out. In protest they kick. In alarm they thump. In play they dance.

What is a bunny dance? Haven't you seen this frolicking series of sideways kicks and mid-air leaps accompanied by a few head shakes and body gyrations? Many rabbits have literally danced their way into human affection.

Thumping, a signal of danger, is not quite so funny. It can be confusing to human house-mates, who don't see any cause for alarm, and it can be particularly annoying to be warned of "danger" throughout the night.

A thump can also be an announcement. We've rescued nursing mothers, who would enter their babies' cage and thump a foot to summon them to dinner.

Herman, our first house rabbit, informed us when things were out of place. She thumped whenever the furniture was rearranged.

WHAT TAILS TELL

The excitement shown by an erect tail can be caused by the threat of an adversary, the proximity of a potential lover, anticipation of petting or treats from a human, or simply the appearance of a new toy in the environment.

In a competitive or a courting context, unneutered rabbits may twitch their tails from side to side and spray their conquests. Although they don't generally see humans as conquests, they may sometimes try to assert their authority by tail-twitching as a form of "back talk" while being scolded.

Theft in the kitchen: Bold Phoebe (left) helps herself to the dry cat chow, while listening (ears rotated) for the bowl's rightful owner.
With an added element of guilt (right), she looks ferocious to ward off a supposed attack.

PHOTOS: TANIA HARRIMAN

"This is a peculiar way of claiming property."

A benignly assertive gesture is chinning. This is a peculiar way of claiming property. By rubbing their under-chin scent glands on the items they're claiming, they mark them as possessions (undetectable to us). Most of the furniture in our house has been claimed and reclaimed by our rabbit occupants and visitors.

TEMPER TANTRUMS

Snorting or growling is a sign of anger. It may be just a warning, or it may coincide with an attack. This kind of anger will not occur unless provoked, and individual rabbits are fairly predictable in what provokes them. When shown gentleness, most rabbits are easy to "mellow out" of an irritable mood.

Cat scratching post?
(opposite) Add to that,
Rabbit chinning post.
Mesmerized:
A few ear rubs puts
Jimmy (right) into a
"presentation" smile.

Pseudo anger is shown by throwing around small objects such as shoes or the food dishes. Most people find this act of assertion amusing.

A comical expression is the shudder. If your hands smell obnoxious (like heavy perfume) when you pet your bunny, he may shake his coat to rid himself of the odor.

EROTIC AND OTHERWISE

Because rabbits draw very little distinction between sexual and social behavior, it's hard to tell which is which. Many expressions are identical. Neutered males and spayed females may still court each other, and they will still run circles around each other and around your feet. Soft "honking" or "oinking" sounds are their love songs. These gestures are also used to solicit food and attention from humans.

A FEW MORE WORDS

In recent years we've identified another vocalization—the whimper. This is a fretting little noise made by a pregnant or pseudo-pregnant female. It means, Please don't disturb me. Also, a rabbit who has not yet learned to trust you may whimper when you try to pick her up or pull her from her cage. Some rabbits "voice" a protest with a few wheezing sniffs, when being picked up and carried.

A more pleasant sound you may hear is the faint "clucking" made by your bunny when given a particularly tasty snack.

KEEP ON SMILING

You've seen it in dogs, why not rabbits? Yes, rabbits have the ability to smile—a whole-body smile. And they can show you several kinds: a sideways flop, an upside-down rollover, or a sedate "presentation." The last one is a common submissive gesture (see page 88), but in this context it's not a tense fearful crouch, but rather, a voluntary submission to the ecstasy of being petted by a favorite human.

PHOTOS: AMY SHAPIRO

Inside Happy Homes

The following examples of rabbits living in human households represent a variety of lifestyles with special problems solved. My husband, Bob, our daughter, Tania, and I visited the homes in our own area. Other interviews were handled by phone and letter.

Readers of the previous edition will recall that this section was arranged according to the control method used: 1) Caged, 2) Confined to one or two rooms, and 3) Unrestricted. We've learned, since the first writing, that those control methods were transitional. Nearly all of the caged rabbits in the last edition had, a year later, earned an open door.

The goal of any house rabbit owner is to have a free-running rabbit, who is never caged, who never gives in to the temptation of chewing furniture and who never has an accident on the floor. This is an achievable goal, but it takes patience from the human and maturity from the rabbit.

Eventually they all can reach "perfection." They may not be show quality, and they may not conform to the standards of their breeds, but all conform to the standards of their human housemates.

PHOTO OPPOSITE: RACHAEL MILLAN-VASTINE. ABOVE: HUGH DOUGLAS

ZELDA: STUDENT AIDE / PHYSICAL THERAPIST

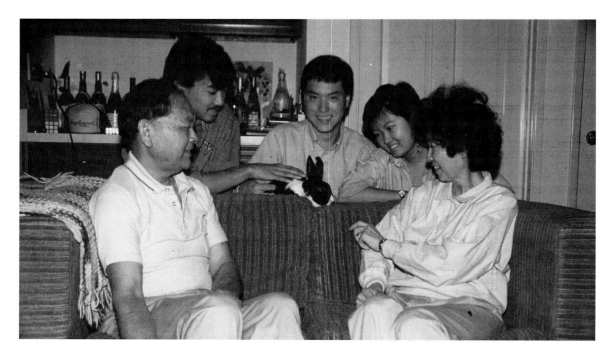

W hat a lot of fuss over such a little rabbit. Zelda is a princess with many attendants. First there's her "owner" (the person legally responsible), Kingstone Shih. And then there's Kingstone's girlfriend, Michelle Okino—and her mother, Edith, her father, Minoru, and her brother, Miles.

All right, who shall we photograph with Zelda? Well, Edith has her hair nuzzled and chewed during evening TV time. Minoru and Zelda share apples. Miles is her baby sitter... Okay, gather 'round. We'll get everybody in.

How did this 3-pound rabbit wind up in this "palace"? It goes back a couple of years to when Bob and I rescued three possibly-pregnant females from the Oakland SPCA.

At that time we had many other rescued rabbits ready for adoption and several prospective adopters to be interviewed. I wasn't particularly eager to return Kingstone's call because he was a student, and that didn't place him at the top of my qualifications list. Yet, my own son was a student *and* a responsible pet owner.

The family portrait (above): Minoru, Miles, Kingstone, Michelle, Edith and of course Zelda, at center stage. Extra indulgence (Opposite): It's Michelle and Kingstone's job.

PHOTO: BOB HARRIMAN

"Tell Kingstone we can't keep his rabbit for him."

Kingstone brought Michelle to help make his selection. They couldn't get past one of my "ladies-in-waiting." I explained that whenever I suspect a pregnancy, I keep the rabbit for 30 days. I suggested making another choice.

I never expected to hear from them again and was surprised when Kingstone called to say he wanted the little black bunny and would wait for her. When the 30 days were up, he called again, and I had to tell him that she had given birth to nine babies and he would have to wait six more weeks until they were weaned. He and Michelle came to visit. Would they want an irresistible baby instead? "I would consider one of the babies," said Kingstone, "if I weren't so taken with the mother."

When the babies were weaned, they all had adopters waiting—and so did the mother. The story might have ended there except for the fact that a student adopter is not in a permanent residence. We could only hope that he had a permanent bond to his pet.

Kingstone's housing changed when he entered graduate school in San Francisco. With Michelle's help, he worked out an arrangement for Zelda. Michelle would look after her in her family's home during the week, and Kingstone would come down to Belmont and take care of her on weekends.

Zelda was not enthusiastically welcomed in the Okino household, especially when she behaved like a normal rabbit in a new environment—a little chewing and a little territory marking, and she was somewhat shy at first. The Okinos were quite dismayed by the idea of

a rabbit in the house. Michelle's father, Minoru, decided to put his foot down. "Tell Kingstone we can't keep his rabbit for him," he instructed his daughter.

About that time Minoru came down with hepatitis and had to be off work for several weeks. He spent many long hours on the couch during the day with no one to look after him except...that's right—Zelda. People who have been treated with animal-assisted therapy know its value. Zelda became a self-assigned therapist and sat daily on Minoru's chest. As he began to recover he thanked her with bits of apple, and a steadfast friendship was formed. All talk of sending her away has been dropped, and only occasionally does she get into a little mischief. She is readily forgiven for unrolling the toilet paper all over the bathroom floor.

TRUFFLES AND SHADOW: THE SHOP BUNNIES

MAYBE HOUSE RABBITS ARE STILL a novelty in Enid, Oklahoma. Or it just seems that way by the look on the customers' faces who come into Steve and Mary Lee Nafus's liquor store. "I didn't know you could bring a rabbit inside," or "I didn't know you could make pets out of them," are comments Truffles and Shadow are used to hearing. Regular customers have grown quite fond of the rabbits, and some say they come into the store only to see them.

When they first get to "work" in the morning, Truffles and Shadow start sniffing for treats, not being the least bit unsettled by the short car trip to the store. They are set up with litterbox and feeding facilities and a large running space. They are never caged and can pretty much do as they please. So going to work every day is just fine with them. Cardboard boxes are present in abundance. All the corners and edges of the boxes can be chewed, and the empty ones provide playhouses. "It's fine for them to chew the boxes," says Steve. "It's only a problem when they chew the price labels off."

Truffles and Shadow are well situated to

PHOTO: MARY LEE NAFUS

"It took her a month to even tolerate Shadow."

spread the good word about house rabbits, and Steve and Mary Lee do all they can to publicize the fact that rabbits can make good housepets. They made a pitch to their neighbors who have outdoor hutch rabbits, hoping to convince them to bring them indoors and get close to them.

Since Steve and Mary Lee lost their first rabbit, Midnight, to uterine cancer, they made it a priority to have their present two females spayed, first and foremost, for health reasons. Another reason was to better the chance of multi-rabbit compatibility.

Here was a case of introducing a female to a female—a task much more

Boxes for all occasions: Truffles (opposite) can chew her boxes, crawl inside, or hop on top. Affection by the pile: Truffles and Shadow (right) share hugs with their human friend, Mary Lee.

difficult than they had expected, especially when they thought they were bringing home a young boyfriend for their year-old Siamese lop. Truffles was indignant over this intruder, and it took her a month to even tolerate Shadow. They had to be housed separately and supervised very carefully when they were let out to run. Shadow, who was smaller, had to be protected from Truffles, who "owned" the territory. Finally, after standing right over them and constantly breaking up fights, Steve and Mary Lee saw their efforts pay off. Truffles decided a rabbit companion wasn't such a bad idea.

Now that they're buddies, the rabbits travel everywhere with their human friends in an air-conditioned car. Mary Lee and Steve had

already been taught by their first rabbit that it's fun to have a bunny along on vacation.

When they stop for refreshments, one (human) runs in to pick up food-to-go, while the other stays in the car with the rabbits. Otherwise they stop in shady rest areas. Truffles and Shadow usually ride loose and sit on the floor of the passenger side of the car, which is equipped with a litterbox. Although food is provided on long trips, they don't like to eat while the car is moving. Sometimes one of them will sit on the seat beside Steve while he is driving.

"There's something very soothing," Steve says, "about driving with a bunny at your side." I didn't think to ask him about his driving record, but I started wondering. If petting a bunny can soothe a driver, would all cars be safer with a bunny on board? At least we might have a society of courteous drivers.

PHOTO: STEVE NAFUS

CELESTE: THE EXPERIENCED TRAVELER

Basket with a view: Celeste observes the scene (upper) from her vantage point in the truck.
Preparing for takeoff: With basket in place, just add the litterbox (lower) for a furnished cockpit. Even the airport breeze (opposite) is familiar.

THE QUESTION THAT WAS GENERATED in Enid, Oklahoma (by phone), I've been able to pursue out here in California. "Do bunnies in the car promote safety and/or more courteous driving?"

"Definitely, yes," answers Joyce Haven, whose bunny Celeste accompanies her on her business. "I drive much differently when Celeste is with me. Normally I'm hyperactive and aggressive, but with Celeste at my side, I'm not harassed by traffic, and I don't feel the pressure to get where I'm going."

Whenever they get stuck in a traffic jam, Joyce says she passes the time by chatting with Celeste.

Not all bunnies would be as thrilled to go as Celeste. Joyce has three other rabbits who are not suited, temperament-wise, to business travel. One of Joyce's business enterprises consists of hauling curly willow and pussy willow in her Ford longbed pickup truck from her garden in Walnut Creek to floral shops in Berkeley. Celeste has been going on these excursions for six years. She rides in her own special basket inside a larger basket to give height (Celeste likes to see out the window). The baskets are wedged into the seat.

Celeste has a fond attachment to her small riding basket. It's her security blanket, and she

PHOTO UPPER: MARINELL HARRIMAN. LOWER: TANIA HARRIMAN

"Not all bunnies would be as thrilled to go as Celeste."

can go anywhere as long as she has her cozy basket. When she goes to the vet, she is allowed to remain in her basket for most of the exam. When they visit a customer, she's carried into the store in her basket. They usually stop for refreshments in a patio coffee shop after their business is completed. Her basket is placed on a chair, where she waits for her order—part of a raisin roll.

Celeste is sociable and very trusting, and she doesn't fear heights—a good thing because Joyce flies a plane, too. The basket arrangement on the seat is similar in the plane.

The trips in the Beech Bonanza are pleasure flights only, and Joyce doesn't fly with Celeste over 8,500 feet elevation. Generally it's no longer than a one-hour trip down to Carmel or up to Mendocino. Joyce takes the litterbox, water and a small bag of pellets.

When Celeste isn't on the road or in the air with Joyce, she's romping in the yard with her rabbit friends. She's the kind of rabbit who likes rabbits and people and enjoys a change of scene. The other rabbits are content to play in the yard by day and rest securely in the house by night, where they have their own bedroom.

PHOTO: TANIA HARRIMAN

LAMBDA, BETA AND KAPPA: TRIPLE FROLICS

AT ONE TIME I THOUGHT it couldn't be done. "Don't even try," I've often advised people who wanted to introduce a third companion to a bonded male-female pair. Well, what did they know in Chicago that we didn't know here? Helen Lau and Franklin Chow were supposed to be novices, and yet they did it. They successfully introduced Kappa, a male mini-lop, to Lambda, their male English spot, and Beta, their female silver-brown mix.

The combination of suitable personalities in the rabbits and persistence in the humans produced this beautiful trio. The essential ingredient in the chemistry is Lambda, the black and white spotted male, who does not threaten other rabbits. He usually approaches other rabbits cautiously and then starts licking and grooming them.

In fact, Lambda gets along with two of the three additional rabbits who have moved into the apartment.

Wait a minute. How did such practical-minded people wind up with six rabbits? (Franklin is a trader at a futures exchange; Helen is a trader's assistant.) Until recently, I hadn't heard the entire story.

I met them, by phone, shortly after they lost their first rabbit in December of '87. Devastated by the loss of their very young bunny, they blamed the tragedy on ignorance—theirs because of improper diet and their vet's because of improper antibiotic (see pp. 75-76). With determination that this would never happen again, they adopted two, a little older, in January '88. (One of these later died with liver disease; the other is Lambda.) It was still a bumpy road for the next few weeks. The bunnies were not instantly affectionate. Housetraining wasn't all that easy, and things were a mess. Helen and Franklin were disappointed and somewhat disillusioned. These were not the model housepets they had read about in the *House Rabbit Handbook.*

A call came from the Anti-Cruelty Society. A baby bunny was available. They had previously requested to be notified, and feeling a little guilty, they decided to take a look at her. They were instantly charmed by the little

"Helen and Franklin spend a lot of time on the floor."

brown bunny, who was more affectionate than their other two. So Beta entered their home.

After all were neutered, Lambda and Beta were introduced by the standard procedures (see Chapter 3) and became fast friends.

As both the rabbit-to-rabbit and the rabbit-to-human relationships blossomed, Helen and Franklin found themselves irreversibly "rabbit people." When they happened across a 4-week-old mini-lop who needed a home, they took him, since they now had both experience and a good rabbit doctor. It was after Kappa was neutered in October '88 that they decided to try an introduction to Lambda and Beta. They readied themselves with gloves and jean jackets and cleared their living room. After carefully supervising a boy-girl meeting with Kappa and Beta, they were more apprehensive about the boy-boy meeting of Kappa and Lambda. Oddly enough, Lambda showed

courting behavior (circling and mounting) rather than aggressive behavior. The boys were separated whenever they started to get too excited, to keep them from winding up in a fight. Finally Lambda began to lick Kappa, which indicated that it was going to work. Two nights later, all three were allowed to run together, but they were supervised for several weeks.

Helen and Franklin spend a lot of time on the floor. Since their rabbits live entirely indoors, they make it a point to exercise them by playing games, encouraging them to run about. Helen says when she wears her long nightgown and they see this "wall" coming towards them, it usually starts them moving.

Helen and Franklin have become experts in three short years. In addition to caring for six rabbits, they have now become volunteer fosterers for the House Rabbit Society.

PHOTO LEFT: HELEN LAU. RIGHT: FRANKLIN CHOW

BAXTER & GINGER-BELL: EASY HOUSEMATES

I MAY HAVE BEEN A LITTLE RUDE at first. Now that Lynda Alston and her husband, Bill Webb, have become two of our dearest friends, we can laugh about it over dinner. "Wheelchair prejudice," Lyndy tells me.

Yes, I had been guilty. The first time she called I tried to talk her out of adopting a rabbit. She has multiple sclerosis. She's in and out of the hospital. How can she possibly take care of a bunny? I was surprised to learn that she and Bill had been living with a house rabbit for nearly four years (in addition to a big sassy cat), and they were looking for a second rabbit companion. I didn't know to what extent Bill was involved in rabbit care or how they had their lives organized. As I later learned, Lyndy does a fair amount of the work, and she has taught me a number of things about organization and saving steps.

In addition to practicalities, however, Lyndy has given me an approach to living that

Toys by the wagon load: Baxter (above) has his pick as well as a place to play under the wagon. Competition for attention: Ginger-Bell (opposite) wants it, too. A reminder is a tug on Lyndy's sleeve.

PHOTO: MARINELL HARRIMAN

"...we were given many updates on how the bunnies were doing."

I have found extremely helpful in dealing with my *outwardly* imperfect animals. I no longer make the assumption that disability means misery. In fact, Lyndy refers to herself as "differently-abled," not disabled.

We didn't make it particularly easy for Bill

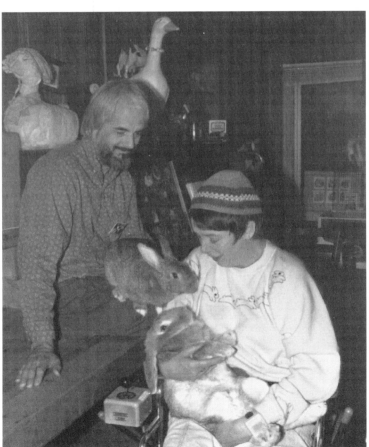

and Lyndy to adopt a rabbit from us. They had to make two trips to our foster home in addition to buying a cage that I recommended from the pet store down the street.

Baxter, their gold mini-lop, was unneutered at the time, so their choice was a spayed female, a 7-pound brown agouti, whom they named Ginger-Bell. Fortunately, her introduction to Baxter required no special handling. It was a rare case of love at first sight (as described on page 86, Plan A).

During the next few months we were given many updates on how the bunnies were doing. And as we got better acquainted, we were able to see how Bill and Lyndy were doing.

Bunny care techniques in this differently-abled household work like this: Bill does all the lifting and any cleaning that requires standing. Lyndy does the rest of the cleaning. She has her rabbit paraphernalia on a lightweight utility cart, which she can push with a little foot power or with her wheelchair to the rabbit cage area. Her supplies consist of newspapers, cat litter, scrapers, trash bags, white vinegar and rags. They invested in a large Superpet cage on legs, because it's easy for her to reach, and the pull-out drawer requires no lifting.

Their studio apartment has no rugs because of Lyndy's wheelchair, so she can keep the hair and occasional "accidents" off the hardwood floors with a Dustbuster or an electric broom. When she needs to get the bunnies back into the cage (when Bill's not home), she lures them in with a trail of treats.

Bob and I were impressed the first time we entered their apartment because it's so pleasant and colorful—like walking into a toy shop. The focus is on fun—a piano, books, oil paintings and such a collection of toys! Lyndy's most recent Christmas present was a chess board with Beatrix Potter bunnies. Then there's a talking Mother Goose that tells fairy tales, a Peter Rabbit music box, and a musical lamp with dancing bunnies. Marionettes dangle from the ceiling (salvaged from a movie director's discards). Her hospital bed is covered with the overflow toys that don't fit in the red wagon (a gift from Bill). Her wheelchair is

covered with bumper stickers advocating animal rights, and her jackets have similar appliques. Over her bed is an exercise trapeze, from which hangs an airplane with a bunny pilot, a Minnie Mouse and a globe.

Lyndy tells me that most people in wheelchairs have colorful living rooms because they spend a lot of time at home and want a cheerful environment. Now I realize that the differently-abled have much to offer a companion animal because of their consciousness of indoor surroundings. More entertainment is provided for Lyndy and Bill's animals, more toys are purchased for them, and more games are played with them.

Baxter's favorite toy is a plastic farmer in a tractor that he likes to push around on the floor. He also likes to play with balls and any rolling object, including his litterbox on wheels (see page 49). Ginger-Bell enjoys tossing more than rolling, so "Mrs. Bunny" was given a set of toy dishes that she can fling about and scatter. Both bunnies enjoy shaking and rattling the plastic baby keys that hang on the side of their cage.

Bill and Lyndy provide the best for their animal friends, who in turn provide great comfort when it's needed. There are times when Lyndy has to be hospitalized, followed by a period of home convalescence. Bill has the job of caring for Lyndy and all of their animals (which now also includes a guinea pig). The animals know their routine and provide Lyndy with maximum pet-assisted therapy just by being there.

PHOTO: MARINELL HARRIMAN

DOROTHY: THE FAMILY PET

PHOTO: HUGH DOUGLAS

AT WHAT AGE SHOULD A CHILD be allowed a pet? This is not an easy question, but I've learned that more important than the age of the children is the commitment of the parents to the training of their children in proper pet care.

It was unlikely, three years ago, that I would let one of my best rabbits go into a home with a toddler and a three-year-old. From the time this wonderful 10-pound lop first arrived in our foster home, we wanted to keep her. I wasn't even planning to show her to Amy Berg and Hugh Douglas when they arrived with their two little boys. We had already turned down several would-be adopters, but somehow I recognized in Amy and Hugh the same priorities as parents that we had years ago. I knew that they would keep close track of their boys' activities with the rabbit. They said it was very important that their children learn about loving kindness and caring. They had already talked to their veterinarian and had put careful thought into making their decision.

It was a perfect match for big, easy-going, affectionate Dorothy. Her size, Amy says, was an advantage against excited little hands.

"...she developed a friendship with each family member."

Before bringing Dorothy home they explained to three-year-old Will that they would *all* be taking care of the rabbit and that his special job was to be gentle and careful.

As Dorothy began to settle in, she developed a friendship with each family member, beginning with Hugh, dancing around his feet every morning and sitting on the couch next to him in the evening, licking his arms. Amy says Dorothy must have known that it was Hugh's idea to adopt her in the first place.

Meanwhile she noticed that Dorothy could often be found lying next to Will on the floor. He enjoyed getting her food, and the baby, Ethan, enjoyed giving Dorothy her daily allotment of crackers. There were times when a contented Dorothy could be seen between the two boys with each resting an arm across her.

Her routine with Amy was during morning coffee-making. Dorothy would tug on her robe or softly scratch on her legs until Amy stooped down to pet her.

Hearing all these stories was gratifying for us, but it would have been unrealistic to

PHOTO: HUGH DOUGLAS

"Amy and Hugh do not take this for granted."

assume that young children growing up would never need to be corrected or reprimanded and that they would know by instinct how to treat an animal.

Amy and Hugh were ready for this when Will's play got too rough with Dorothy. He was promptly restricted from playing with her for two days. Amy explained to him that rough play was harmful to Dorothy, and that he would have to watch how Mama and Papa treated her.

Will was enthusiastic about handling Dorothy when his two days were up, but several weeks later he forgot the warning and was again playing too roughly with her. This time he was restricted for four days, which impressed him with the seriousness of treating an animal gently. There has never been another incident, but Amy and Hugh do not take this for granted. "The foremost responsibility to make sure she is handled properly is mine and my husband's," says Amy.

Both boys have learned to give Dorothy careful attention. Her willingness to lie close to them and be caressed is their reward. Dorothy retires to her cage at night after she has been given an hour of attention on Amy and Hugh's bed. She's truly a family pet.

What makes it all work is evident in Amy's words, "We put about as much thought into expanding our family with a new animal as we would to expand it in any other way." As important as forethought is commitment to permanence, and I'm very proud to show their recent portrait (page 17), taken three years later.

PHOTOS: HUGH DOUGLAS

DARLA: THE OFFICE ASSISTANT

MANY HOUSE RABBITS SPEND their days in home offices—an incongruity considering their penchant for cord chewing. Graphic designers with home office/studio combinations have a few hundred extra cords to worry about, since most contemporary designers work with computers and an array of peripherals. Darla lives at Kifer Graphics with her two humans, Kathy Kifer and Don Latarski of Eugene, Oregon.

Darla is a beautiful black and white rex with magnificent fur. She is the only pet in the household and the second rabbit.

Their first rabbit had lived in a hutch in the backyard with a guinea pig. When he caught pneumonia later in his life, he moved into Kathy's office in the house. After seeing how nice it was to have him inside she knew, after he died, that she wanted her next one to be a house rabbit.

Darla is much more spirited than her first rabbit (no two are alike). She uses her teeth a lot more and occasionally lunges and snarls.

Trust re-won: Lap-sitting for Darla (above) had to be earned by Kathy. Being picked up doesn't mean "back-to-the-cage."

PHOTO: DON LATARSKI

"...Darla jumps onto Kathy's back for a ride around the room."

But she loves to be stroked and will sometimes flop over contentedly on her side. Outside during play time, "she leaps tall boulders, zigzags around shrubs, runs flat out on the straightaway and stops on a dime—a creature truly designed for escaping predators."

The yard is fenced, but Kathy still keeps an eye on Darla through the glass walls around her studio, and she's not even allowed outside unless Kathy is going to be home for a while. It's too hard to catch her. As Kathy explains, "She leads me through all the shrubs and every spider web in the yard. It's easier on both of us if I can wait for her to come to the door on her own." Kathy makes it a point not to put her in the cage immediately when she comes in.

Kathy and Don are avid gardeners but have found that Darla does surprisingly little damage. She munches mostly on dried leaves and "only takes one bite of everything else."

She spends her daily down-time in her cage near Darla's desk. In the evening Don's music studio is closed off (it has still more tempting cords), and Darla can run in the rest of the house. Although she is getting much better, Darla is not allowed on the couch, because she couldn't resist "marking" it. So usually Kathy joins her on the floor. Sometimes Darla jumps onto Kathy's back for a ride around the room.

Kathy learned an important lesson in rabbit psychology. She used to pick her up to carry her back to the cage at bedtime, and Darla associated being picked up with back-to-the-cage, which made her more difficult to pick up. Now Kathy refrains from betraying her trust, and she herds her and bribes her at bedtime. After taking a very circuitous route, Darla scoots into her cage, where a treat is waiting. She's now willing to lap-sit again.

Darla's behavior is improving, but she has taken some nibbles on woodwork and a few chair legs. Kathy's books on the lower shelves took a beating, so she moved her less important magazines there. Darla's litterbox is filled with alfalfa hay, which gets dumped every day into the compost bin.

Darla provides plenty of entertainment for Kathy and Don and their friends. "She always gets a laugh by racing through the living room at full throttle—just a blur of fur, ears back and leaning in on the corners." And, as any house rabbit owner would corroborate, "Sitting up on two feet always gets an 'awww' from anyone in the room."

PHOTO : DON LATARSKI

SHAUNEE: CO-TENANT OF HUMAN SPACE

CREATIVE PEOPLE ARE OFTEN rabbit people. Maybe it's because they are a little more open-minded to divergent lifestyles. Carol Molly Prier, a Berkeley ceramicist, raised Shaunee in her third-floor apartment without the aid of a cage. She chose a rabbit companion because she felt that this would be an animal who could be happy in that amount of space.

When Shaunee started to cut his teeth on the furniture during his adolescence, Carol Molly held steadfast to her anti-cage principles and offered more, more, and more chew-ing alternatives. Her best solution was to give him disposable grass mats for his own use. One time she spilled molasses on his rug, and as much as she tried to clean it off, he was delighted with his chew-toy. Less tasty toys come from garage sales. When she noticed him in a shoe-chewing stage, she supplied him with his own pair of baby shoes.

Whenever she needs to section off a room, she uses expandable window screens that she can simply step over and he can see through.

Techniques can be found to meet just about any need in a human-rabbit household.

A laissez-faire setting: Nothing is ever forced against Shaunee's will. This includes lap sitting, but for brief moments he can tolerate it.

PHOTOS: TANIA HARRIMAN

BR´ER AND BACI: GIFTS TO THE CARING

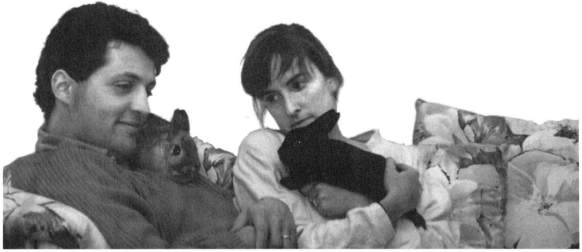

TWO TINY TREASURES WERE rescued from the Marina Sanctuary in West Los Angeles. First little black Br'er moved in with Mary Alice and Ron Mita. A few months later, during extremely hot weather, these caring people noticed some less-caring people drop off a little gray bunny at the Sanctuary.

"We can't leave her here," Ron said.

And so, the short-eared, chinchilla colored Baci moved in with Ron, Mary Alice, and Br'er. From their little teachers, these humans had to learn a lot more about bunny-proofing than they did from their first rabbit, who had a malocclusion and didn't do much chewing.

Ron had been dating Mary Alice for five years before he surprised her with their first bunny for Christmas. "Ron knew of my obsession with rabbits," assures Mary Alice, knowing that it's a risk to surprise someone with the gift of an animal (often these are not welcome surprises). Also, Ron obtained approval from all eight women who lived with Mary Alice in off-campus housing in New York.

After Ron and Mary Alice married and moved to California, they lost their bunny to an intestinal blockage—a condition they didn't yet know how to prevent.

The pair they have now are definitely in love. They like toys with bells and lots of noisy things. They like to use them when their human housemates are trying to sleep. On a normal day active time is at 7:00 p.m. The bunnies run for about an hour and investigate the home-office, where a heavy-duty, office-cord concealer wraps all around the room.

Accounting, homework, and bill-paying are done on the floor so that time can be spent with the bunnies. I think most house rabbit owners do the same. I receive many letters with nibbles out of the corners.

PHOTO: PAUL KNAPP

PROFESSOR TOBIAS: CHIEF ADVISOR

IT WAS HARD TO BEGIN to talk about the O'Connell rabbits because there are nine of them, and each one is special—Captain Bandit, Sir Dandy, Mrs. Maggie, Papa Smooches, Mademoiselle P'hoppy, Professor Tobias, Cossette, Ambassador Max Factor, and their last family-addition, Jet Doenut. Each one is distinctly and vastly different. One may be cuddly; one may be aggressively playful; one may be calm and mellow.

All of their bunnies get a fair amount of attention (a remarkable accomplishment, considering their number). This is possible largely because Cheryl and Ken conduct their insulation business from their Buffalo, New York home. The office is just a few steps away.

"Not everyone needs to enjoy house rabbits in that quantity," I said. "Surely, you have one who's a little extra special." Well, yes, Cheryl admitted. Professor Tobias is the only one who has unrestricted run of the house. He never liked a cage and was not forced into one.

His day starts by jumping onto the bed to wake up Cheryl and Ken. When they're not feeling well, Tobias is extra attentive, and he was even there to help out one time when Ken was having a bad dream.

No matter where he is in the house, Tobias knows his name and comes running when he's called. Cheryl usually carries cracker or cereal treats around in her pockets and doles them out as needed. Tobias makes a thorough inspection of both hands before he believes the snacks are gone.

Vantage points: From his podium (left) Tobias can make his announcements. A better place to be is on a lap (opposite) when there's cake to be shared.

Tobias has a few favorite blankets that he likes to sprawl on. No matter where his blankets are, that's where he will nap. And like a few of the more outgoing rabbits we've known, he likes a resting spot with a visual vantage instead of a secluded place under a bed.

Cheryl and Ken are working on getting compatible pairs established so that all their bunnies can be out to run for longer periods. At present they take turns running in a large carpeted rabbit room where their cages are set

PHOTO: CHERYL O´CONNELL

"All of their bunnies get a fair amount of attention."

up and lavishly furnished with toys.

The O'Connells found a good buy on carpet squares, which they can pick up and wash. They installed a glass panel on the door to the rabbit room so that they and the bunnies can keep track of each other at all times. Their reason for installing central air-conditioning was for their bunnies' comfort. One of them, Sir Dandy, is a Jersey Wooly who particularly likes to stretch out over a vent in the summer and let his hair fly.

One of the most amazing things about Cheryl and Ken O'Connell as rabbit owners is that they never mention the workload of caring for nine rabbits. All I hear are marvelous stories telling of the wonderful things their bunnies do, of their intelligent problem-solving feats, and of their ability to provide constant entertainment. Cheryl says, "We've seen bunnies pout, get mad, silly with joy, overcome with affection, and act indignant."

I wonder if they expected this much when Ken and Cheryl got married in '89 and decided that *a* rabbit would be their housepet.

TAYLOR: THE SENIOR GENTLEMAN

WE TOLD HER TO HAVE SOME FUN with the project. Our daughter, Tania, set out on a Sunday morning, camera in hand, to shoot some rabbit people. All we knew about them was that Tania bunny sat for them while they honeymooned in Europe last fall. And, oh yes, there were several times before that. It was Melinda who left Tania her car while she was away so that more of Tania's time could be spent with the rabbits and less on the bus. Melinda Bascone and Richard Dow are what Tania describes as "very particular" about the way their bunnies are treated.

The recipients of these attentions now number four rabbits, but out in the lead with personality and seniority is a gorgeous 7-year old black bunny named Taylor. Taylor's running space is the bedroom; his mate, Jessie (not shown), is rather shy and more inclined to be under the bed than on top of the bed. Taylor is always available, though, and doesn't mind having his picture taken. By all accounts, Taylor is a real people rabbit—cuddly, affectionate, and responsive.

Closer all the time: Taylor didn't have to work very hard with Melinda. She has been appreciating his qualities for the past seven years.

Richard says when he first met Taylor, he had a "typical male" reaction. He thought the bunny was cute, but he didn't quite understand this intense relationship Melinda had with her rabbit. He was even surprised to see him running around the apartment. Taylor had moved into Melinda's student apartment while she was a sophomore at U.C. It took Richard about six months to really warm up to him, but they eventually became very close.

They took in Jessie, a fuzzy lop couple of

PHOTOS: TANIA HARRIMAN

"...when he first met Taylor, he had a 'typical male' reaction."

years later, when Melinda got out of school and went to work. She was spending less time at home, and they didn't want Taylor to be lonely. The two rabbits were getting along well, when Buster came along. Buster, a five-year-old lop, was a depressed bunny from an abusive situation. With good care, he recovered from the multiple infections that afflicted him and became another personable rabbit. When it became apparent that the three rabbits could not be housed together, the apartment was divided into two sections. When Buster appeared lonely in his section (which includes the living room), Melinda and Richard adopted Greta, a gold mini-lop, from the House Rabbit Society.

Another victory: Taylor finds it was worth his time to teach Richard how to be responsive. Now he has a second who pampers him.

They had seen how gratifying it is to watch a bonded pair of rabbits. They now wanted Buster to have the same kind of companionship as Taylor. After the second rabbit they didn't notice so much additional upkeep. "We have it down to a routine," says Richard. They gave their bunnies new, easy-upkeep cages for Christmas and removed the doors. The rabbits are free-running and use their cages as bedrooms.

Melinda and Richard belong to many animal-welfare organizations. Richard has more to say about their relationship with their animals because he has been through the greater transition. Melinda he says always had rap-port with animals, and he aways "liked" them. But it was the depth and intensity in Melinda's relationship that so amazed him. It was after his own first six months with Taylor, that he began to see how this could happen .

HERMAN: THE HOUSE SUPERVISOR

This is the only story from the first edition that I've taken the liberty to repeat. The reason is obvious. Without Herman the House Rabbit Handbook *would never have been written (at least not by me).*

BARGING INTO OUR LIVES uninvited, Herman changed what we thought about rabbits. With a manner that was smug and complacent and intelligence that rivaled a dog's, she took over our house and never gave it back.

Herman spent two years with us before an intestinal problem took her life. We wish it could have been longer, but what she gave us in those two years is still with us.

As you may have guessed, we thought she was a he when we first found her in the backyard, but by the time we discovered our error, she knew her name as Herman.

At fourteen pleasing pounds, she was big in every way—size, character, personality and heart. She carried an enormous dewlap under her chin, and one ear sort of lopped. Her legs were too short for her large, stocky body, but so what? To us she was beautiful.

Her sense of propriety was startling. Of course there was only one right way to pick her up, but she also knew how the furniture should be arranged and where everything should be placed. This trait made box-training a snap.

She was confined to the kitchen at first but gradually took on the whole house. For chewing control we did a bunny-proofing job on our house and offered plenty of alternative toys. We tried to keep her out of our bedroom, but she was very persistent.

By six months old she would sneak into the bedroom and become so exhilarated over her victory that she would turn our bed into a trampoline. We were so amused that we let her have it during the day. We continued to put her in the kitchen at night while she continued to insist on sleeping with us. It took another six months before she won. We had to adjust to having our faces licked every ten minutes all through the night. It did occur to me to turn over, but I'd usually find that she was standing on my hair and had me pinned to the pillow.

Generous with favors: Herman warms our hearts with her kissess (left) and cools her belly on the hearth (right).

KEEPING SCORE

Her propriety showed in her fairness to Bob. When it was the correct time for him to

PHOTO: MARINELL HARRIMAN

pet her, she would lick his hand and then shove her head under it. I can't claim she counted, but after a given number of strokes, it was her turn to lick him again.

In seeing that things were properly done, she supervised all household activities from fixing the washer to sorting out magazines and left the distinct impression of evaluating it all.

Propriety could be mixed with mischief, as she would grab a newspaper out of our hands and run with it. After a few times chasing her around the room, we realized it was the atten-tion she wanted, not the paper, and she knew how to get what she wanted. "You cheat," I often told her. "You manipulate me with your charms, and it's not fair."

At times she was downright sneaky, but her guilt was revealed by her tail. I would walk by her without realizing that she had pulled a book out of the bookcase, until I saw her tail twitching defiantly.

Some behavior may never be explained. One incident involved our cat, Nice, who was engaged in the not-so-nice activity of torturing

Bed sharing:
In deep slumber with Bob (left), Herman wakes in competion for my lap (right).

a mouse. She would turn the mouse loose and let it almost get away, then pounce on it just before it was out of sight. Herman observed this demonstration and thumped her foot in protest. When the protest was ignored, Herman attacked the cat from behind and knocked her off her feet, allowing the mouse to escape. I had mixed emotions over the episode. A minute before, I was pitying the mouse. Now I was concerned over it being loose in the house. Then I pitied Nice for not knowing what on earth had provoked that attack from Herman. Then I began to wonder what had gone on in Herman's little head. Why had she protected a mouse? Do animals preyed upon feel an alliance against predators? This is something I will probably never know.

The whole family used Herman for stress reduction, and at times I even questioned the idea of pets being child substitutes. Sometimes our roles were reversed, and she was a parent, or grandparent. She may not have wiped away tears with her apron, but she could certainly soothe and comfort us and assure us that things were okay.

Having her with me at all times in my home office/studio seemed the natural way to conduct my business. She had added such a new dimension to my life that I felt I had grown an extra limb. When I lost her, I may have been less of a freak, but I felt like an amputee.

I must confess to a psychological bondage. We took her with us in our heads to many places where one would not expect to find a rabbit. A dinner party guest, seated next to one of us, was usually unprepared for the conversation, "Oh, you haven't heard of our wonderful rabbit? Well, let me tell you..."

PHOTO ABOVE LEFT: MARINELL HARRIMAN.   PHOTO ABOVE RIGHT: BOB HARRIMAN

WHY AN INDOOR RABBIT?

THE PRECEDING CHAPTER gives examples of human-rabbit households. All of the rabbits shown live indoors with their human friends. This does not mean that they never go outside to play, but it does mean that their home base, or warren, is in the house. My main reason for emphasizing this idea is that it's very hard to really know an animal who is not part of your own ambiance. Can you really give as much time to an outdoor pet? Not unless you sleep outside, eat your meals there, and conduct your business from an outdoor phone. Getting close to your companion animal requires putting in the time, and if you're a busy person, this is hard to do—unless your time serves double duty. You can do a lot of routine tasks while socializing your rabbit, and you can have the best of both worlds.

Aside from the psychological benefits of keeping a rabbit indoors, there are physical reasons to have even an outdoor rabbit inside at night. City dwellers are usually unaware of the predators that threaten outdoor rabbits. The most commonly underestimated rabbit predators are raccoons, who come up through storm drains into very urban areas and find prey at night. Other predatory animals include stray dogs, feral cats, large birds, and—in more rural areas—foxes, wolves, and large reptiles. Another little known fact is that the presence of a predator in the vicinity (within distance to be seen, smelled or heard) can be enough to trigger a terminal state of shock before teeth or claws have even touched the rabbit.

If your bunny is a house rabbit, you won't have to worry about those unpleasant things, and you can concentrate on important matters like your relationship.

Expectations

By Holly O'Meara

MY OPPORTUNITY TO work with an ongoing number of rabbits has heightened my expectation for an individual rabbit. As a child, I wanted every small animal to submit to and lavishly return my attentions. Often, I was disappointed. I remember a baby rabbit, handled from birth, who nevertheless "didn't like me."

Later, as an adult—when I least expected it—one confident, expressive rabbit came into my life. She changed my mind forever about what a rabbit can be.

Now it's up to me to encourage these traits in every rabbit I meet. The "mean" rabbit, the "scared" rabbit, and most of all, the rabbit "who doesn't like people," are stereotypes that dissolve when these rabbits are treated as individuals with the potential to change. ᴖ

FOR THE COMFORT OF ALL

IF YOU FEEL you can no longer live without a house rabbit, you will want to know how you can live *with* one. Most of us who have been through the process of training our rabbits and ourselves have groped for answers. We had no one to turn to for advice. Books on so-called pet rabbits gave us recipes and pelting procedures, not house-training techniques or chewing-control methods.

No longer alone, house rabbit owners can recognize one another. Having been duly initiated, we proudly wear the labels of our rabbits. Our belts, purse straps and shoelaces are chewed, and the corners of our briefcases bear similar marks of distinction. To join this elite group you are required to have a sense of humor. It will help you through times of vexation. The other times you will handle with common sense, instinct and what you have learned from other "rabbit people."

Our examples in the previous chapter were to show that rabbits can live in human households. This chapter deals with "how to."

PHOTOS: AMY SHAPIRO

THE NITTY-GRITTY OF TOILET TRAINING

THE FIRST MATTER OF CONCERN to people with any indoor pet is housetraining. Actually, rabbits train themselves. Your job is to encourage this natural tendency.

Rabbit feces, consisting of vegetable fibers, are not as odorous as that of cats or dogs. A few stray hard "marbles," which can be easily swept up, are a minor nuisance rather than a major disaster.

Urine, which can damage floors and furniture, is much more important to control. Begin with confinement and add freedom as it's earned. The easiest way is to start with a cage, even if you hope to discard the cage eventually. Otherwise a small room or section of a room will do. Place a litterbox in the corner of the cage that your bunny chooses for a "bathroom." If she chooses several areas outside the cage, then set up several litterboxes. This is not forever. As bunny matures she will narrow her choices to one or two favorite places. Multiple litterboxes achieve results much faster than verbal reprimands, and they're easier to clean than the carpet.

Good toilet habits may take weeks or months to achieve, depending on maturity. Don't expect a perfectly housetrained bunny at 6 weeks. Older rabbits are often easier to train because they're more willing to settle into a routine.

If a mishap results in a wet rug, sponge it with white vinegar. This is an outstanding cleaner. The high alkalinity of rabbit urine is neutralized by the acidity of the vinegar. It removes both urine stains and odors.

It's advisable to keep bunny off the beds and upholstered furniture until a litterbox habit is well established. A soft cushion may feel too much like soft litter material.

Also, bunnies like to mark new territory when they're let out to play. If you take them straight to a large litterbox from the cage, they soon get the idea that the litterbox is the territory to mark, and they associate it with their freedom. Within a few weeks, you can open the cage door, and they'll make a beeline for the litterbox on the floor.

REPROGRAMMABLE

An entrenched habit can be halted by making a drastic change in routine. For instance, we rescued 4½-year-old Nora from our local shelter. She had never been housetrained. In our house she chose a very inconvenient (for us) bathroom in front of our closet door, where I couldn't place a litterbox. We started over.

PHOTO: AMY SHAPIRO

"The choice is between the soft litter and the wire cage floor."

She went back to the cage for several weeks, and her running space was restricted to a play pen. Then I carefully reintroduced her to our bedroom by carrying her each time from her cage to the litterbox in the corner of the room opposite the closet. She now uses the box consistently, on her own, and has entirely forgotten the area in front of the closet.

SUGAR COATING THE PILL

"Pill" control is more difficult for some rabbits and depends largely on individual metabolism. Rabbits who drop their pills while they're eating can be fed in the cage or on a tray. Some will sit for long periods of time in the litterbox and take care of their grooming at the same time. This should be encouraged. Make the litterbox a pleasant place; never use it for punishment.

Some people are disturbed at seeing their rabbit sleep in the litterbox. Unlike cats, rabbits do not regard their feces as "dirty," and the choice is between the soft litter and the wire cage floor. The simple solution is to offer your bunny an alternative bed such as a second box or a washable synthetic-sheepskin rug from your pet supply store.

CAUSES OF SLIPUPS

There are a few occasions in which even the best trained house rabbits may temporarily forsake their good toilet habits. The most common causes are:

1. Hormones. Unneutered males and unspayed females may leave their "trademarks,"urine or feces, around to make an impression on the animal (or object) that

they're trying to seduce. Spaying or neutering is advisable for many reasons. This is one of them.

2. Competition. In multi-animal households, some rabbits may scatter droppings to show competitors whose territory it is. Once a pecking-order is established, the problem diminishes.

3. Excitement. Even neutered compatible rabbits, when getting acquainted, have about a 2-day period that we call a "honeymoon," which results in looser bowels and an untidy floor. We confine honeymooning couples to a rugless floor during this period.

4. Illness. A rabbit with real diarrhea (and listlessness) needs immediate medical attention. Also, if a housetrained rabbit begins to urinate on the floor, there's a good chance of a bladder/kidney infection. In both cases consult a veterinarian.

SUPPLIES AND SETUP

BOWLS, BOTTLES, FEEDERS and hay bins—equipment for the front end—come in a wide variety. I use them all. Water bottles and bin feeders that hang outside the cage work best where space needs to be optimized. Water bottles should be checked daily for leakage or plugging. A wire coat-hanger is perfect for dislodging stuck balls in the ballpoint tube.

Bowls for food and water can be used wherever space is not a problem. Plastic bowls should have an extra-wide lip that can't be gripped in bunny's teeth and turned over. Pet supply stores have very nice heavy clay bowls for pet use, but if you shop elsewhere, have pottery checked for lead content.

SUPPLIES FOR THE OTHER END

Every house rabbit owner wants bunny's bathroom to be clean and odor-free, with the least amount of effort. Some people feel that it's easier to clean out a litterbox than a whole cage. Others bypass a litterbox altogether and have bunny use just the cage. Still others keep up both cage and litterbox, because cleanings are less frequent.

The sizes, styles and number of litterboxes depend on space requirements and individual habits. The cage-size training box can be as small as 9″ x 12″. It's real purpose is to reinforce good habits that will extend to free time outside the cage. Note: small litterboxes can be tipped over unless they're fastened to the cage with pony clips or small wire ties.

We used to be open-minded about what to put in the litterbox, but experience in the House Rabbit Society has limited our choices. First, litter must be non-toxic if ingested. Rabbits will often chew their litter. A popular choice in the past was wood shavings, but because of the phenols they contain (which cause liver damage), we don't use them in any area where there's prolonged inhalation of the fumes. Rabbits linger much longer in their litterboxes than cats and are more at risk.

A few extras:
Foot padding can be added (left) with a washable rug.
A variety of toilet styles (opposite) are used inside or outside the cage.

Good alternatives, now available in pet supply stores, are Cat Country Organic by Mountain Meadow Products and Cat Works by Purina. Another is an aromatic orange peel litter by Blossom Products. A lightweight cardboard-type litter is made by Absorption Corp. If your local pet store can't get you any of these, you may have to settle for dustless clay.

PHOTO: MARINELL HARRIMAN

"...litterboxes depend on space requirements and individual habits."

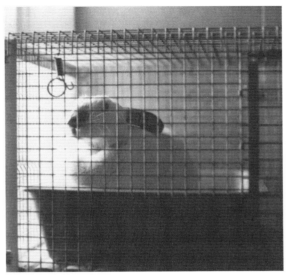

PHOTOS LEFT, LOWER RIGHT: MARINELL HARRIMAN. UPPER RIGHT: BETTY TSUBAMOTO

HABITATS BOUGHT AND BUILT

THE OPTIMUM LIVING ARRANGEMENT for a house rabbit is one that is integrated into your own lifestyle. Basic physical requirements can be met with just about any adequately sized, basic cage, but if that's as far as you take it, all you will have is basic boredom. Don't accuse your rabbit of being dull-witted.

Think of what will be around the cage as well as what will be in it. Placement of the cage or living quarters is as important as size. Will it be isolated in some area where your bunny never sees you or hears you talk on the phone, or will it be a part of your own furnishings in an area where you can share experiences?

STORE-BOUGHT CAGES

You may plan a custom habitat in the future, but it's advisable to start with a store-bought cage so that you can see what features work best. The size of the cage should depend on how much time is spent inside it. The longer the time, the larger it should be.

Look for a cage with at least one large door,

Integrated environment: Rabbit business and human business are conducted together at Kifer Graphics. A cage in a home office can add relationship opportunities to career opportunities.

PHOTO: KATHY KIFER

"Top-opening doors should be at least half the length of the top."

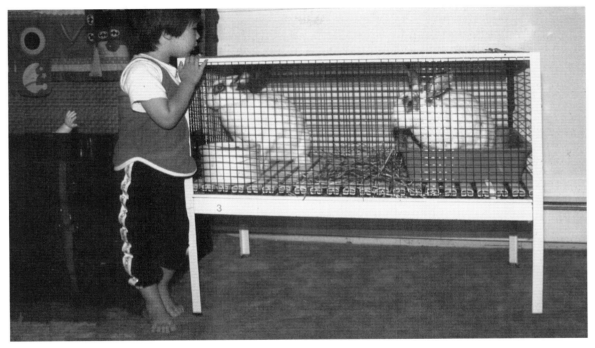

On higher legs: Young children have unlimited observation, yet a top opening means that Mom lifts the bunnies out at playtime. This insures that their activities with the children can be supervised.

the bigger the better. Litter-boxes, toys, food bowls, and sometimes a reluctant bunny have to be pulled through that door. Top-opening doors should be at least half the length of the cage (preferably the whole top opens). Most rabbits, large and small, can hop in and out with ease (proof on page 16). An extra safety precaution is to spread a towel over any area where a toe might get caught in the wire. A cage on legs

must have a side door if you want bunny to get in and out on his own. Some models have both side and top openings.

Side-opening models often have a small door. You can enlarge it with wire clippers. Cages with side or front doors provide more flexibility in furniture arrangement, because they can be placed under tables or shelves.

A cage with a slide-out tray is much easier to clean than one that has to be lifted off the tray. The tray catches all the debris and spillover from the cage litterbox as well as the accumulated hair and hay from the cage floor.

"It can be a simple solution or highly imaginative..."

Once your bunny has reliable house habits, you may be able to remove the cage entirely. If she really likes her cage and needs a place to call her own, you may want to either remodel her store-bought cage or design one to fit with your decor. It can be a simple solution or highly imaginative—as the ones shown here.

A TWO-STORY SOLUTION

Because a new rabbit (in a house with several) had a long wait for her turn at running-time, Terry and Jesus Valerio built her a spacious habitat against a wall in their family room (shown above). The upper level, with an overhang, is 58"L x 28"H x 29"D. Materials are 1 x 2 pine and 1" welded wire. It has multiple doors, including a special side door where Terry can pull up a chair for a visit. A ramp connects the two floors.

A SPLIT-LEVEL SOLUTION

Carolyn Long of Milwaukee designed an L-shaped bunny condominium, of wood and hardware cloth, to fit under her pottery/toy shelves. It has three removable doors, and the main "hall" is 36"H. The total depth is 54", and the width at the back is 69". A metal pan from a dog crate covers the hall/dining-room.

PHOTOS: TERRY VALERIO

Above: Bunny condo with the front door removed. In the foreground is the dining room. A half-level up is bathroom #1. Up and to the right from there is the play loft (seen through "carved" bars). Underneath the loft is bathroom #2 (with a larger litterbox), connected by an archway to the cave room underneath bathroom #1. The cave also has an entrance on the left side of the condo. Right: Top view of the condo in its environment.

Cages in Home Decor

By Judy Morin

AFTER SEVERAL EXPERIENCES *with our house rabbits, my husband came up with an ideal cage. He has made several of them for new rabbit owners. The top opens for your convenience, and a full side door, for your pets' convenience, opens outward with a detachable ramp. Size and color can be of the owner's choice to match the decor of their home. Our experience has been to make them 31"H x 18"D x 36"W to house the smaller rabbits. Each cage is constructed with hardware cloth, never chicken wire, to prevent the rabbits from hurting their teeth on the wire. Also, hardware cloth is more comfortable on their feet. Splash rails are installed, and the bottom pan slides on rails for easy cleaning. Legs can be cut to any height.* ☙

PHOTOS UPPER: CAROLYN LONG. SIDEBAR: JUDY MORIN

HOW TO SAVE YOUR HOUSE

RABBIT DISCIPLINE, OR SUPERVISION, consists of a sharp "No!" or a clap of your hands or a stomp of your foot—anything that startles, but it can't be used if there's no one there to enforce the discipline. Protecting your bunny and your possessions is better done by bunny-proofing. Prevention is much less costly than repair.

The extent of bunny-proofing will depend on what kind of mischief your rabbit decides to get into. Usually it will be only one or two particular places that I call "problem areas." The cause can be something as simple as a cookie crumb deep in the carpet that attracts digging or chewing. The smell of damp wood on a rainy day might also stimulate chewing.

Not all house rabbits respond the same way, and you will certainly not require all of the bunny-proofing material I'm suggesting. These are simply some devices that have been tried and work for many.

1. Plexiglas: A small sheet from the hardware store can cover a problem area of linoleum, hardwood floor or even a wall. It's transparent, and you can hardly tell it's there.

2. Repellants such as Cat Away can be sprayed on soft or hard material. Don't overdo. It only takes a tiny bit. Rabbits take one sniff and turn the other way. Some perfumes may also be effective. My daughter's favorites are positively disgusting to our rabbits.

3. Tabasco sauce may discourage a few rabbits. However, others find it palatable.

4. Bitters prepared by your pharmacy for thumb-sucking problems in children. Experimentation will indicate which works best on your rabbit, but I have learned that any deterrent has to be sprayed or rubbed on daily.

Unscathed living rooms: The trick to house protection (left and right) is to follow the suggestions for bunny-proofing and chewing alternatives.

Perhaps when the manufacturers of pet products realize our needs, they will come up with an effective, harmless chewing repellent for our house rabbits.

5. Wooden bumpers: A thin strip of untreated wood can be tacked onto a baseboard. It not only protects the baseboard but provides a chewing block. If you need a flexible covering, garden aluminum, in 4″ wide rolls, can be cut with scissors to any length and tacked or stapled over problem areas. We use this on our wooden porch.

6. Plastic tubing: Sold in hardware stores for about 18 ¢ a foot, it can be slit lengthwise,

"Prevention is much less costly than repair."

and with an electrical cord shoved inside, the tubing closes right back around the cord. It's easy and discourages most rabbits from even attempting to chomp the wire.

7. On-wall plastic casing. Complete with elbows (sold also in hardware stores), it can protect phone cords with a finished look and does not detract from room decor.

8. Furniture arrangement. This is also a way to hide wiring. We have too much furniture stuffed into a small house, and we can place a piece of furniture or even a waste basket over practically any problem. We buy cheap, unfinished straw waste baskets.

9. Blanket throws. For protection against toenails and teeth, a large towel or a throw can be tossed over upholstery or beds. These items can take everyday wear and be removed when you're expecting company.

10. Grass mats. An inexpensive, disposable (organic) rug can be laid on top of any frayed section of a more expensive rug. This is a great diversion for cat clawing as well as bunny chewing.

11. Murphy's Oil Soap. To prevent and/or repair urine stains on hardwood floors.

PHOTO: AMY SHAPIRO

TOYS FOR TEETH AND TOES

THE MATERIALS MENTIONED in the last section are to prevent chewing. On the other hand, rabbits need harmless chewables to satisfy their gnawing instincts. Inside your house we call these materials alternatives, since they are given in place of forbidden items. House rabbits derive great pleasure from their toys, which provide chewing, digging, shaking and general entertainment.

Here are a few suggestions:

1. Straw of all kinds is more appealing to bunny than your other furnishings. Be generous with this. You can buy it in the bale, loose, or woven into baskets or rugs. Straw helps with digestion as well as recreation.

2. Cardboard boxes and paper bags serve for crawling inside, scratching and additional chewing.

3. Newsprint paper or paper towels are fun for shredding with teeth and feet. Although printers' ink no longer contains lead, it smears, so unprinted paper is a cleaner choice.

After a carrot sample the sofa:
This bale of furniture (above) is all right to nibble on.
Joys of paper products: (opposite) Dive into a paper bag or a paper cup. (The bag is a better fit.) Crawl inside a cardboard box or chew it up.

PHOTOS: BOB HARRIMAN

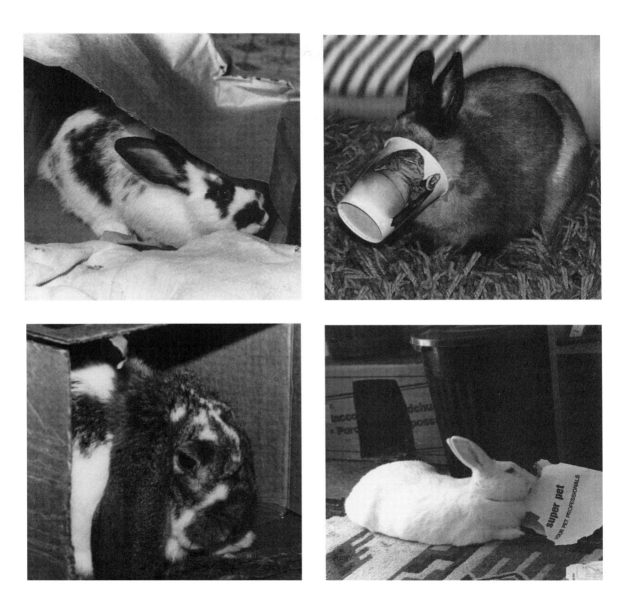

PHOTOS UPPER LEFT: TANIA HARRIMAN. UPPER RIGHT & LOWER LEFT: MARINELL HARRIMAN. LOWER RIGHT: AMY SHAPIRO

A good workout: Minnie blasts through her carpeted tunnel (left), a perfect full-body exercise toy. Daphne exercises (middle) from the neck up with her toss toy. Thumper (right) assumes that the dried flowers are chew-toys.

4. Wood. Untreated scrap wood or firewood with bark make good chewing, as well as small tree-branches. Exceptions are cherry, peach, apricot, plum and redwood, which are listed by poison centers as toxic.

6. Binzo bones, or other cereal based chew-toys for dogs are also enjoyed by rabbits.

7. Nudge-and-roll toys can be large rubber balls or cylinders, such as empty salt cartons, toilet paper spools and noisy, clanky soup cans.

8. Toss-toys keep bunnies busy. A favorite is Batta-Bout, a metal ball of rings, which bunny can pick up and toss or nudge and roll.

9. Mason-jar lids are a more recent discovery. Give one to a bored rabbit inside a cage and watch what he does with it.

10. Baby toys of hard plastic, dangling inside the cage, provide noisy, shakable fun.

11. Tunnels of any kind are enjoyed by rabbits both indoors and outdoors. A carpeted cat tunnel encourages indoor exercise and provides an outlet for bunny's energy.

12. Digging boxes are useful for rabbits with excessive digging needs. These are simply deep cardboard boxes or plastic tubs lined with paper, straw or litter. This gives bunny something to dig into other than your carpet.

13. A towel on a smooth floor gives a bunny something to scoot around, bunch up, and unfold again—for recreation.

Kay Leiker of Wichita, Kansas has researched toy shopping, and her advice is that you observe what your rabbit likes to do. Usually it's "nudging things, picking things up in their mouths and shaking or throwing them, moving things with front feet (somewhat like cats do) and chewing." She also advises no sharp edges, loose parts, or soft rubber that can be chewed into small bits and swallowed.

You can find harmless entertainment for your house rabbit that can satisfy just about any mental or physical need.

PHOTO LEFT: BILL YADEN.   MIDDLE: MARINELL HARRIMAN.   RIGHT: MARK LICHTENFELD

PLANTS NOT FOR CHEWING

House and garden plants are chewing-temptations, but domestic rabbits do not know by instinct which to avoid. The following are toxic in varying degrees.

African rue
Agapanthus
Alder buckthorn
Alsike clover
Amaryllis
Anemone
Angel's trumpet
Anthurium
Apple (seeds)
Apple leaf croton
Apricot (all parts except fruit)
Arrowgrass
Arrowhead vine (oxalate)
Asparagus fern
Autumn crocus
Avocado leaves
Azalea/Rosebay
Balsam-apple/Balsam-pear/Bitter gourd (berries)
Baneberry/Doll's eyes
Barberry
Begonia (sand)
Betel nut palm
Bird of paradise
Bittersweet/Horsenettle/Woody nightshade
Bitterweed
Black locust/Acacia (inner bark, young shoots)
Black nightshade berry
Black Root
Black walnut
Bladderpod
Bleeding heart/Dutchman's breeches (foliage, roots)
Bloodroot
Blue cohosh
Bluebonnet/Lupine
Boston ivy
Boxwood
Bracken fern

Branching Ivy
Broomweed/Snakeweed/Turpentine weed
Buckeye/Horse chestnut (young shoots, seeds)
Buckthorn/Fireweed/Fiddleneck
Buddhist pine
Bull nettle
Bunchberry
Burroweed
Buttercup/Ranuncula
Butterfly weed
Cactus thorn
Caladium
Calamondin orange tree
Calendula/Pot marigold
Calico bush//Mountain laurel
Calla lily (oxalates)
Candelabra cactus
Cardinal flower
Carnation
Castor bean/Palma Christi
Century plant
Ceriman
Cherry (all parts except fruit)
Chinaberry tree (fruit)
Chinese Lantern/Chinese bellflower/Flowering maple
Chokecherry (wilted leaf)
Christmas rose
Cineraria
Clematis
Cocklebur
Coffeebean/Senna-bean (seeds)
Coral berry
Cordatum
Corn cockle
Corn plant

Cottoneaster
Coyotillo/Tullidora (berries)
Creeping Charlie (except houseplant)
Croton (see apple-leaf)
Crown of Thorns
Cuban Laurel
Cutleaf Philodendron
Cycads
Cyclamen
Daffodil (bulb)
Daisy
Daphne (berries, bark)
Deadly Nightshade
Death Camas (bulbs)
Delphinium (seeds, young plants)
Desert Tobacco/Wild Tobacco/Indian tobacco
Devil's ivy
Devil's tomato/Silverleaf
Dogbane/Indian Hemp (leaves)
Dracaena palm/Ribbon plant
Dragon Tree
Dumbcane/Charming dieffenbachia/Giant Dumbcane/Tropic Snow
Dutchman's Pipe
Elaine
Elderberry (roots, stems)
Elephant ear
Emerald duke
Emerald feather
English ivy (ilex acid)
Eucalyptus
Euonymus
Exotica perfection
Eyebane
False hellebore
False parsley

Fiddle-leaf Fig
Firecracker
Florida Beauty
Fluffy Ruffles
Fly poison/Staggergrass/Crow poison
Four O'Clock
Foxglove
Foxwood
Fruit Salad Plant
Garden sorrel (oxalates)
Geranium (California)
German Ivy
Glacier Ivy
Gladiola
Glory Lily
Gold Dust Dracaena
Gold Toothed Aloe
Golden Pothos
Goldenchain
Greasewood
Green Gold Nephthysis
Groundsel/Rattlebox/Rattleweed/Wild pea
Guajillo
Halogeton
Hawaiian Baby Wood Rose
Heart Ivy
Heartleaf
Hedge Apples
Henbane, black
Hogwort
Holly berry
Horse-Head
Horsebrush
Horsenettle/nightshade
Horsetail Reed
Hyacinth (bulb)
Hydrangea (blossom)
Indian laurel
Indian Rubber plant
Indigo
Inkberry

🐰 🐰 🐰 PLANTS NOT FOR CHEWING

Inkweed/Drymary
Iris (rhizome, leaves)
Ivy (Boston, English, Hahn's self-branching)
Jack-in-the-pulpit/ skunk cabbage
Jerusalem cherry
Jessamine/Wild jasmine (night-blooming)
Jimmy fern/Cloak fern
Jimson weed/Thorn apple/Jamestown weed
Johnson grass
Jonquil (narcissus bulb)
Juniper
Klamath weed/St. Johnswort/goatweed
Lambkill/Ivy bush/Laurel
Larkspur (seeds, young plants)
Laurel (English)
Laurel cherry
Lechuguilla
Lily of the Valley
Lobelia
Locoweed, Milkvetch, Crown vetch
Madagascar dragon tree/ Red-margined dracaena
Maiden Hair tree
Majesty
Marble queen, Silver pathos (oxalates)
Marijuana
Marsh Marigold/Cowslip
Mayapple/Mandrake
Medicine Plant/Aloe vera/True aloe
Mescal Bean/Frijolito/Mountain laurel
Mesquite
Mexican Breadfruit
Mexicantes
Milkweed
Miniature Croton
Mistletoe

Monkshood/Wolfsbane
Moonflower
Moonseed
Morning glory/Flying saucers/Pearly gates/ Heavenly blues
Mother-in-Law
Mushroom
Mustards/Crucifers/Cress
Needlepoint ivy
Nephthytis (oxalates)
Nutmeg
Oak (acorns, foliage)
Oleander/Rose bay
Orange sneezeweed
Oxalis, Shamrock plant
Panda
Paper-flowers
Paradise plant
Parlor ivy
Parsnip
Partridge breast
Peach (leaves, twigs, seeds)
Pencil Cactus
Peony
Perill mint/Beefsteak plant
Periwinkle
Peyote/Mescaline (cactus tops)
Philodendron
Pigweed
Pingue/Colorado rubber weed
Plumosa Fern
Poinciana (seeds, pods)
PoinsettIa
Poison Ash
Poison hemlock/California fern/Fool's parsley
Poison Ivy
Poison Nut
Poison Oak
Poison Sumac
Pokeweed/Pokeroot
Poppy (except California)
Pot mum/Spider mum
Potato (green parts)

Pothos (oxalates)
Precatory bean/ Jequirity bean/Rosary bean
Prickly copper-weed
Prickly Poppy
Primrose/primula
Privet/Ligustrum (berries, leaves)
Pyracantha berry/ Firethorn
Rattlebox/Purple sesbane
Rayless goldenrod
Red clover hays (moldy)
Red emerald
Red princess
Red sage (unripe berries)
Rhododendron
Rhubarb leaves
Ripple Ivy
Sacahuista/Beargrass
Saddle Leaf Philodendron
Sago Palm
Sand Begonia
Satin Pothos
Schefflera
Scindapus
Seed pits: almond, apple apricot, cherry, peach, pear, plum
Sesbane/Bladder pod/Rattlebox
Silverling/Baccharis/Yerba -de-pasmo
Skunk cabbage/Corn lily
Snake Palm
Snow-on-the-mountain
Solomon's Seal
Sorghum/Sudan grass/ Kafir/Milo/Schrock
Spathe flower
Spathiphyllum
Split leaf philodendron
Spotted Dumb Cane/ Variable Dieffenbachia/ Gold dieffenbachia
Sprengeri fern (asparagus)
Squill

Star of Bethlehem
Stinkweed
String of beads/pearls
Striped Dracaena
Swamp Laurel/Bog Kalmia
Sweet pea
Sweetheart Ivy
Swiss cheese plant
Tallow, Japanese/Chinese (leaves, berries)
Tansy ragwort/ Groundsel/Senecio
Taro Vine
Toadstools
Tomato (leaves, vines)
Toyon/Christmas berry/ California holly (leaves)
Tree Philodendron
Tree tobacco
Trumpet Plant
Tulip (bulb)
Umbrella plant
Variegated Philodendron
Variegated Rubber Plant
Victoria Regia
Violet seeds
Virginia creeper/woodbine
Walnut (green shells)
Warneckei Dracaena
Water hemlock/poison parsnip
Weeping Fig
White snakeroot
Wild carrots
Wild cucumber
Wild parsnip
Wild peas
Wisteria (seeds, pods)
Wood-rose
Yaupon holly/Cassine (berries)
Yellow jasmine/Carolina jessamine/Evening trum- pet flower
Yellow star thistle/Yellow knapweed
Yew (berries)

OUTDOOR PLAYPENS

ADEQUATE PHYSICAL ACTIVITY for your rabbit can be achieved indoors, but you may at times want to get her out for some fresh air. If you simply turn her loose in the backyard you may not find her when you want to bring her in.

Many people think that rabbits must be allowed to dig in the dirt, but there are cleaner, safer ways to provide for digging needs. In city neighborhoods, most backyard dirt has been contaminated with bacteria that are harmful to rabbits. When clouds of dirt are dug up and inhaled by your rabbit, it could result in lung damage and pneumonia.

Left: A playpen under construction. The frame, usually of pine or fir 2 x 4s, is 8′ L x 32″ W x 32″ H. Right: Jeremy and Melissa take turns with Charlie in this safe daytime enclosure.

THE PORTABLE RUN

The solution that we have worked out for our foster rabbits is to build playpens of 1″ welded wire, stretched over wooden frames. The wire covers all four sides and the bottom. The wire floor is covered with a thick layer of clean yellow straw. The rabbits can dig, burrow, push and shove without risking their health.

The 8′ length gives them enough room to kick up their heels and run around. Yet the whole frame is not too heavy to turn over for cleaning or to move about the yard. Plywood tops should be latched, not hinged, so that they can be completely removed for cleaning.

THE PORCH PEN

Elizabeth TeSelle of Bloomington, Indiana worked out a different solution for her three rabbits. She didn't want her two angoras to pick up leaves and sticks from the yard.

By attaching a wire dog-pen to a cage she had on hand, she formed an area 4′W x 6′L x 4′H on her shaded porch, where she can keep an eye on them. The cage serves as a shelter where the bunnies can hide if a car pulls up or they get nervous.

PHOTO LEFT: BOB HARRIMAN. RIGHT: ELIZABETH TE SELLE

TRAVELING ON FOOT

SINCE WE HAVE BACKYARD playpens, I seldom use a harness and leash except for traveling. When we stop in a rest area and the harnesses are put on, our bunnies start to anticipate getting out for a run. They have learned to associate the harness with playtime, and there is no resistance to this strange encumbrance.

My rabbits do fine with figure-8 harnesses and light chain leashes, but people who walk their rabbits more regularly prefer other types. I keep my leash fairly short and held high to keep from entangling around small shrubs.

Rabbits panic when trapped in a tangled leash.

Kari S. Gilje of Seattle, Washington has written an article on exercising rabbits and sent us some useful advice on the harness and leash. She prefers a nylon webbing harness sold for small dogs because she feels a plain collar and a figure-8 tend to tighten too much around the neck. Her Holland lop, who weighs 5 ½ pounds, does well with the smallest size dog harness, but she recommends taking your rabbit to the pet store to try on a few for fit.

The leash should be one that can't easily be chewed through (she makes her own from mountaineering-type rope). Also, extendable leashes on a reel are ideal for rabbits' sporadic hopping. The best models for rabbits are ones designed for cats or small dogs. No leash should ever be left on a rabbit unattended.

Anyone who has gone through leash lessons with a rabbit will be amused by Kari's description: "...rabbits usually won't walk on a leash like a dog, so people will think you are strange when they see you running in spurts, first this way and then that way. Rabbits make you pay attention! They like to suddenly take off when you are not ready. Then they come to an abrupt halt."

When you visit a well-cultivated public park, find out if chemicals have been sprayed recently on the lawn or other plants. Going for a walk with your bunny is an excellent option for apartment dwellers who have no access to a backyard. It's less demanding than walking a dog twice a day, every day. And it's always fun to watch a bunny play.

PHOTO: BOB HARRIMAN

TRAVELING ON WHEELS AND...

M Y DOG LOVES TO GO for a ride; my cats abhor the idea. Most of my rabbits endure a car ride better than my cats, and some actually enjoy the outing. Unless your bunny accompanies you to work, there will be fewer occasions that require putting bunny in the car.

Maximum comfort depends on how far you will be going. Generally, you will need some type of ventilated carrier. Pet supply stores sell cardboard box-type carriers with top opening which are fine for getting bunny to the vet and for short trips around town. If you plan on more extensive travel, it's a good idea to invest in a sturdy carrier such as a Kennel Cab. They're convenient to handle and the ventilation holes are on the sides, not on top. This is preferable for rabbits, because they seem to feel more secure with a solid roof overhead.

EXTENDED CAR TRAVEL

When we are planning to be on the road for half a day or more, we set up a cage for our bunnies, so that they can stretch out. It's advisable to strap cages and carriers inside the car in case you have to come to a sudden stop.

One of the greatest problems in car travel with any animal is dealing with summer heat. Ice blocks inside or wet towels across the cage, along with ventilation, can cool bunny down—while the car is moving. The problem is when you have to stop. You can't leave a rabbit in a car parked in the sun.

We have often had to pass by restaurants and go hungry until we could find a place to park in the shade. If you must travel with your

bunny during the summer heat, try to plan it for early morning and late evening.

AIR TRAVEL

It may be surprising to the airline industry to deal with rabbit owners who insist that their rabbits have the same rights as cats and dogs. Some airlines don't allow rabbits on their planes at all. Others allow them only in cargo. A few of the more enlightened airlines allow rabbits in carriers in the cabin with you. Inquire before making your reservation. The more requests to take rabbits in the cabin, the more airlines will realize the growing demand.

If rabbits are allowed only in cargo, ask about temperature and pressure control. Also, you may want to have your bun delivered to you by hand after you've landed, rather than passed down the conveyer belt. Each airline is different, so check first about carrier requirements, health certificates and any pet services they provide.

WHEN BUNNY DOESN'T TRAVEL

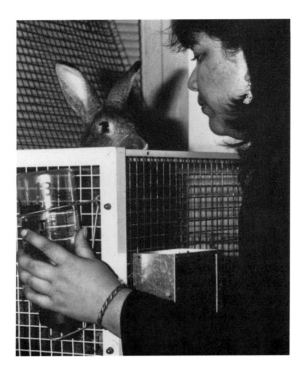

A friendly exchange: Pet sitters should be able to establish rapport with your pets as well as to keep them clean and well fed.

YOUR TRAVELING PLANS may not always include your rabbit. An out-of-town convention might be difficult to attend with a bunny along. Or you may be traveling outside the country, and going through customs and quarantines could be disastrous. What are your alternatives?

Obviously, your first choice would be to ask close friends who already know your rabbit to look after him in your absence. The better your friends know your rabbit the easier it will be for everyone. But if you live alone in a new area, you may not yet have friends nearby.

The next best thing to having a bunny-sitter who knows *your* rabbit is to have one who knows rabbits. You may want to start by asking your vet for referrals for either a reputable boarding kennel or a pet-sitting service. A variety of services are available. Check on what suits your needs best. Some do actual house-sitting. Others will come in at specified times to feed and exercise your animals. Others may board your animal on their own premises. If you choose boarding, you will of course want to see the facilities. Check for kennel cleanliness and ask about exercise accommodations.

Competent pet-sitters are familiar with health needs of the species that they're working with. Most are experienced at giving injections and can follow any program that your vet has prescribed.

Two examples of pet-sitters in my area are my daughter, Tania, who learned about rabbits by helping us foster, and Charlie Esple, a former state humane officer.

Tania's clients have come about informally through word-of-mouth referrals. She boards rabbits, a few at a time, in her apartment and also does some house sitting. Prior to accepting the responsibility to care for a rabbit, Tania requires a signed check from the owner made out to the veterinary hospital, in case of an emergency. Instead of frightening people

"...important is the time he takes to sit quietly or play with the animal."

away, this policy has caused owners to relax—so much so that I recommend the same for anyone who must leave and animal in the custody of someone else. The unexpected can happen at the most inconvenient times.

Charlie's experience as an officer taught him to calm a frightened animal and how to go from being a stranger to being a friend in a short period of time. This skill serves him well, both as an HRS foster parent and as a pet sitter.

His pet sitting services include nuts-and-bolts tasks, such as cleaning the litterbox, bringing in the mail and newspapers, and watering plants. Equally important is the time he takes to sit quietly or play with the animal.

His means of letting people know he's there is by veterinary bulletin board. In your own area, this might be the place to look for a pet sitter. Also, pet supply stores and humane societies have bulletin boards to check. You should be able to find a number of free-

lancers, with good recommendations or large organizations with local branches. Locating someone that you like and your bunny likes means freedom for you to travel without guilt.

The Natural Rabbit

By Amy Shapiro

As the creature in charge of food, water, shelter, and toys, I'm your basic meddlesome human. Almost every aspect of my rabbits' lives is the result of some decision of mine. I try to make choices based as much as possible on what is natural for them, to help them feel at home in this human place.

I choose to neuter/spay my rabbits even though mating and reproduction are very natural. Social interaction with other rabbits is an equally primary instinct, one that I could not provide for an unneutered bunny. The choice here is not between natural and unnatural but between two sets of natural behaviors.

A cage is an unnatural object, but it may also be a stepping-stone to greater freedom, so the rabbit can ultimately make a few choices for herself.

Our companion rabbits are not wild animals. For better or worse, we have taken that kind of naturalness away from them. Now it is up to us to re-define the boundaries, using all our nosy, intervening human nature to make it the best of all possible worlds. It's the least we can do for them.

To A Longer Life

4

OFTEN THE QUESTION IS asked, "How do rabbits manage in the wild?" The answer is, "They don't"—stay alive, that is. Most wild rabbits don't make it through their second year.

Our domestic rabbits can live 8-10 years, as we continue to push longevity limits. Obviously, we're not interested in livestock solutions, such as, "Destroy the sick rabbit to save your herd."

Left: Bandit finds this exam a bit too thorough for comfort. Right:Begging bunnies are hard to resist. We may overfeed, but the advantage to a vigorous appetite is that changes are noticeable.

What is the best course for the individual pet owner? Rather than memorize names of diseases, learn how your rabbit's body works and what is normal. Spend time studying your rabbit. What is normal behavior? Posture? Appetite? Temperature? What are normal skin color and coat condition? What are normal droppings? Noticing changes in time to get treatment may be what will keep your bunny alive.

PHOTO OPPOSITE: BOB HARRIMAN. ABOVE: MARINELL HARRIMAN

DINING-ROOM MENUS

BASIC HEALTH CARE BEGINS with diet. Yet, no single diet is perfect for all ages and all conditions. In general, young animals require more calcium and more protein, but in excess, these may contribute to urinary disease in older animals. Pet-food companies now manufacture "senior" dog and cat foods, so hopefully bunny chow will follow. Although it's possible to give your rabbit a balanced diet without pellets, it's very difficult, and you should first be an expert in rabbit physiology as well as a knowledgeable nutritionist.

It's easier to start with good-quality rabbit pellets (16-20% crude fiber; 14-18% protein) and adjust to individual needs. Buy pellets as fresh as possible (within 3 months of milling) and store them in a cool dry closet. Moldy or rancid pellets can kill a rabbit. Dr. Richard Evans (see endnotes) advises, "Stay with a nationally known company that has tested its product on rabbits. Do not be afraid to contact the company and ask what data they have to back up their product."

If you ration pellets, have your vet determine Thumper's ideal weight and give you a feeding chart. You can feed to maintain ideal weight (e.g., 9 tbl. pellets/6 lb. body weight).

GOOD FIBER HABITS

A daily handful of hay aids in the mechanics of digestion and helps prevent many intestinal disorders. Legume hays, such as alfalfa and clover, are very rich in protein and more appropriate for younger rabbits. Older, and overweight rabbits, can be offered grass or oat hays or straw, the non-nutritive stem part of a crop. If your rabbit is on high-fiber pellets, less hay can be given.

TREATS

In addition to knowing *what* treats to give a rabbit, you need to learn *how much*. Introduce new foods gradually (for very young bunnies see page 81). Go easy on starchy treats such as crackers, pretzels, cereals and even rolled oats. A sudden overload of starches in the hindgut can upset digestion. If you're going to indulge your bunny in these treats, give a small amount daily, not a large quantity once in a while. Mine get a daily handful of rolled oats or a cracker. Many rabbits enjoy crunching on toasted sourdough bread.

The youngster (opposite) with a wistful sigh must wait a few weeks before he is allowed to taste the oat treats inside the jar.

Fresh vegetables and fruit can be offered in small to moderate amounts. At the first sign of diarrhea, cut back. My "ok" veggie list includes: carrot, broccoli, parsley, radish tops, watercress, mint, cilantro, and sometimes leaf lettuce.

Avoid, as regular treats: spinach, cabbage, cauliflower, rape, kale, and mustard. These are high in either *oxalate*s or *goitrogens* and are toxic in accumulated quantities over a period of time.

Never offer a rabbit raw beans, potato peels, rhubarb, or any scraps that are too old to eat yourself. Your rabbit is less able to tolerate stale fare than you are. Fruit and vegetables needn't be at room temperature. Cold food is far safer for a rabbit than spoiled food.

PHOTO: BOB HARRIMAN

"Gnawing on wood doesn't mean bunnies can eat anything."

Peel fruit or wash with soap unless you know that pesticides have not been used. Most fruits, with the exception of banana (not overly ripe), have the potential to cause diarrhea so start small. Fresh pineapple, papaya and kiwi contain beneficial enzymes (discussed on page 73). Rabbits love raisins, but be cautious with these—also with cookies and other sweets. Excess sugar can cause the same problems in the intestine as excess starch.

INTESTINAL FRIENDS

A worthwhile diet additive is lactic acid, which promotes the growth of "good" bacteria in the large intestine. The most available form is in acidophilus, liquid or powder. Lactobacillus acidophilus is a beneficial bacteria culture that produces lactic acid. It does not replace bad bacteria but provides an environment for the growth of good bacteria. Natural yogurt is a source of acidophilus and

can be given. I generally add powdered acidophilus to drinking water (100mg capsule/pint water). That way I don't have to remember to give it in "doses."

THE BALANCED FLORA

Some natural and necessary rabbit behavior may give some false impressions. Gnawing on wood doesn't mean bunnies can eat anything. They have a delicate bacterial balance in the large intestine and cecum. A rabbit relies on anaerobic bacteria (grows without oxygen) in the cecum to break down cellulose. The cecum is a pouch-like structure of the large intestine (see page 71). It can digest cellulose, which the small intestine can't do. The products of this cellulose fermentation (volatile fatty acids) are absorbed into the blood for nutrients. The cecum also packages special little "vitamin pills" to be reingested (synonymous with cud-chewing in ruminants). Maintaining a healthy cecum is crucial for survival. This large fermenting vat, activated by dietary fiber, must support beneficial bacteria and protozoa in order to do its work.

If the microbial balance of the cecum or large intestine is altered, not only will this halt digestion, but it will produce the growth of detrimental organisms—many producing highly toxic substances that can kill the rabbit. This is precisely why you are being cautioned not to overload your bunny with starches or sweets. The basic problem is imbalance. This is also why certain drugs must be avoided. They destroy the beneficial bacteria and allow the harmful ones to overgrow (see page 75-76).

PHOTO: MARINELL HARRIMAN

The Digestive Path of the Rabbit

Food processing in a rabbit depends heavily on a large fermenting vat (cecum) in addition to the small intestine, shown as follows:

1. Plant food, ground by the rabbit with a sideways motion of the lower jaw, is swallowed and passed to the stomach through the esophagus.

2. Muscular contractions squeeze and churn the food in a circular path, separating food particles and mixing them with the gastric fluid of the stomach.

3. As the food particles exit the stomach, enzymes produced in the pancreas, as well as fluid produced by the liver, are secreted into the small intestine at the duodenum.

4 The major part of digestion takes place during passage through the small intestine. Most protein and starches are absorbed, while cellulose passes to the cecum.

5. Undigested materials enter the cecum, where they are separated into large and small particles. Larger particles are eliminated; smaller particles are sent to the large fermentation vat.

6. Bacteria produce B-complex vitamins and digest cellulose and any remaining protein and starch not digested in the small intestine. Volatile fatty acids are produced which are absorbed into the blood.

7. Undigested fiber and waste (hard droppings, or fecal pellets) pass through the large intestine along with vitamin-rich soft droppings (cecal pellets).

8. Cecal pellets are consumed directly from the anus and returned to the digestive system.

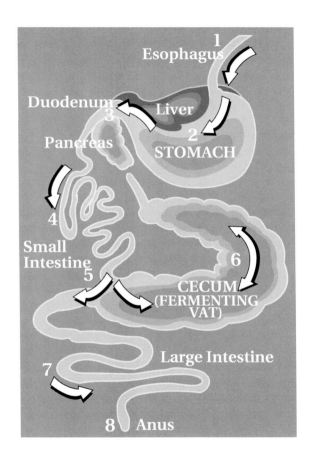

INHABITANTS OF THE GI TRACT
Stomach & Small Intestine: Sterile (kept sterile by certain fatty acids found only in goats, coconuts and rabbits)
Large Intestine & Cecum: Fermentation flora—composed of protozoa and anaerobic bacteria (both gram-positive and gram-negative as explained on page 75).
Specific types of bacteria are:
    Bacteroides sp (gram-negative)
    Streptococcus fecalis (gram-positive)
    Clostridia sp (gram-positive) some are very harmful.

DIGESTIVE DILEMMAS

A HEALTHY DIGESTIVE TRACT is an active one. As shown on page 71, all swallowed material has to move through a very long digestive path. When the action shuts down, you have a very sick bunny. Digestive interruptions can alter intestinal flora, which in turn can lead to enteritis (inflammation of the intestine) or to enterotoxemia, a deadly disease caused by toxin-producing bacteria. Digestive interruptions have a number of causes. You're already preventing one of them by sensible feeding. Other causes may be parasites, such as coccidia (intestinal or hepatic), stress of any kind (including environmental stressors), intestinal blockage, bacterial or viral infection, or any sudden change in diet.

ENOUGH TIME?

Signs of intestinal disturbance—diarrhea, bloat, mucus in the stools, and sometimes constipation—may show before a bunny "acts sick," and treatment can be prescribed before

Palpation: Experienced hands, feeling in the right places, can often detect major internal problems.

the illness advances to a toxic state. Once pathogenic (harmful) bacteria take over, they can produce toxins that cause death in a very short time. Remember that bacterial imbalance in either the cecum or the large intestine, whatever the cause, is potentially lethal to your rabbit. If your bunny shows any of the signs and is listless, get him to the vet *immediately*.

OF LESSER WORRY

Instead of an acute illness, your bunny may have a chronic disorder that recurs regularly or even occasionally. You may experiment with:
1. acidophilus (see page 70)
2. digestive enzymes (tablets or powder)
3. electrolytes (from the vet or Gatorade)
4. purified water
5. increase/decrease fiber
6. decrease vegetable/fruit treats
7. change pellet brands

We have tried all of the above but seem to get the most consistent results with enzymes. We use Prozyme powder (¼ tsp./day) sprinkled on the pellets. It's sometimes easier to give it in unsweetened applesauce (2 tbl.).

FOR LONG HAIRS AND SHORT

Another possible disorder of the GI (gastrointestinal) tract is wool block. Rabbits, like cats, are meticulous groomers, but unlike cats, rabbits are virtually unable to vomit. Any swallowed hair has to move downward through the stomach and extremely long intestine. Accumulated hair that doesn't

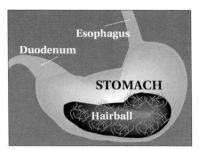

Figure 1: Partial Stomach Blockage. Food consumption is reduced but not stopped. Can be treated at home under veterinary directions.

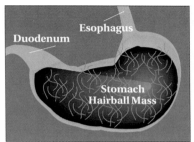

Figure 2: Entire Stomach Blockage. Prevents food intake. Must be dissolved or surgically removed. Stomach can rupture.

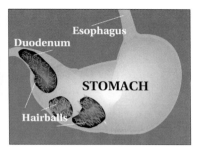

Figure 3: Intestinal Blockage. Partially broken fur mass enters the small intestine but does not pass through it.

move can form life-threatening furballs in the stomach or in the small intestine.

An experienced veterinarian can usually detect a blockage through palpation (feeling the abdomen), but x-rays may also be necessary. If treatment to dissolve and pass the furball is unsuccessful, your vet may have to resort to surgical removal.

The most common prevention is a 1½-inch strand of vitamin-fortified cat laxative about twice a week for rabbits over 7 months. Also, papaya/pineapple (papain/ bromelein) enzyme tablets are helpful. Enzymes do not dissolve hair protein (or stomach lining) but instead digest pellets and gelatinous mucus that bind hair together. Once the hair is loosened, it can pass through the digestive tract. The most palatable are the generic supermarket brands. We give 5 or 6 tablets a day to medium-size rabbits. The strength we use is 45mg bromelain, 30mg papain.

Multiple enzymes (mentioned earlier), such as Prozyme or Nutrazyme, have been tremendously successful with some of our rabbits as both hairball and enteritis preventives.

Another technique for preventing furblock is to remove pellets one day a week. People who use this method generally give hay and vegetables on that day. My own variation is to do it daily rather than weekly (to avoid abrupt dietary changes). Since my foster rabbits go into exercise runs every day, they are away from their pellet bowls for 6-8 hours, at which time they have access to straw, hay, and water.

I can't ration pellets. Our rabbits live in groups and eat ad libitum (free choice) when they're inside at night. Of 76 rabbits, only one (very inactive rabbit) is obese, and we haven't had a furball case in over 5 years.

My conclusion is that daily exercise significantly helps prevent hairballs and breaks the boredom that leads to excessive fur chewing.

FIGHTING INFECTIONS INSIDE AND OUT

ALTHOUGH A FEW VIRUSES have been identified in rabbits, more is known about rabbit diseases that are caused by bacteria. Vaccines are not usually available for these. To complicate matters, some of the more common bacteria (such as Pasteurella or E. coli) carried by other species can be particularly troublesome in rabbits.

This does not mean that you can't let your rabbit play with your cat, provided there isn't a lot of biting and scratching going on. If you do notice a wound from any source, promptly grab the Xenodine and disinfect it.

WHO GIVES WHAT TO WHOM?

When interviewing prospective rabbit adopters, I'm sometimes asked by concerned parents, "What diseases can the children pick up from the rabbit?" Amusedly, I reply, "It's more likely that the rabbit will pick up something from the children."

I base this comment on the assumption that my children were normal and that most school-age children are exposed to many "bugs" on the playground (and hygiene is not instinctive until they reach their teens). Well, reasonable hand-washing, among the humans, can keep a household bunny from excessive exposure to a variety of bacteria.

BACTERIA BEHAVIOR

An animal's immune system is usually able to defend against invading bacteria by producing antibodies that destroy them. But when the animal is stressed, physically or psychologically, the immune system is down, and opportunistic bacteria can get a foothold. The immune system is then unable to adequately cope with the bacteria that cause infection. When this happens to your rabbit, you may be warned by any of the following signs:

1. Runny nose/eyes, sneezing
2. Labored breathing
3. A head tilt, incoordination
4. Limb paralysis
5. Incontinence (urine-soaked bottom)
6. Fever (normal is around 102°F)
7. Local swelling, inflammation
8. Pus anywhere
9. Loss of appetite

A rabbit infection may take one of several courses. The first (and worst) is that it may become septicemic and spread via the blood from a less critical location to a vital organ. (A toe abscess and pneumonia may be caused by the same bacteria.)

Another course is that it may become walled off where it can't be "seen" and destroyed by the immune system and where it can't be penetrated by antibiotics. A walled-off infection may eventually rupture and spill its contents into surrounding tissue and then become septicemic. Bacteria, even from a walled-off infection, may slip through small sinuses to form adjacent pockets.

TREATMENT

When an abscess occurs in an area close to a surface where it can be lanced and drained or surgically removed, it is mandatory to do so and not leave a possible "time bomb." Treatment needs to be aggressive and persistent. A local disinfectant, such as Xenodine can be applied at the site, and a systemic antibiotic is often given to prevent septicemic spread.

More difficult to reach are infections in bony tissue, the nasal cavity, the brain, inner ear, lymph nodes or any internal organ. These must be treated with a hardworking systemic antibiotic.

DRUGS: GOOD AND BETTER

The choice in drugs for most animals is simply made by culturing the bacteria and finding their sensitivities. It's not so simple with a rabbit. Your veterinarian has to prescribe medication that will destroy the infection without destroying the intestinal bacteria necessary for your rabbit's digestion.

Bacteria are classified into two groups, gram-positive and gram-negative, by special stains. Both reside in the rabbit intestine (see page 71), but drugs with predominantly gram-positive spectra can upset the bacterial balance. The most commonly used, potentially dangerous (to rabbits) antibiotics are of the penicillin family, especially Amoxicillin and

ANTIBIOTIC THERAPY FOR PET RABBITS

The following table of successful antibiotic treatment is based on data from several branches of the House Rabbit Society over a two-year period. All drugs were prescribed by our veterinarians, and all rabbits were monitored for side effects during treatment.

Some rabbits had acute illness. Others were chronic, and some went from acute to chronic. Some infections changed cultures, and drugs were changed accordingly. Not all infections were totally eradicated, but if they were sufficiently suppressed to allow the animal a normal life, we considered the treatment successful.

Table 1. The safest antibiotics for rabbits

DRUG	BRAND/COMMON NAME	NUMBER OF RABBITS	DURATION OF TREATMENT MINIMUM	MAXIMUM
Sulfanomides with Trimethoprin	Ditrim (injectable)	20	10 days	3 mos.
	Septra, Tribrissen Bacterin	50	10 days	1 mo.
Chloramphenicol Chloromycetin	Chloro	15	14 days	2 mos.
Quinolones	Enrofloxacins (Baytril)	6	3 wks.	6 wks
	Ciprofloxacin	25	5 days	1 mo.
Tetracycline	Oxytretacycline (oral)	30	10 days	2 yrs.
	(injectable)	5	1 mo.	2 mos.
Gentamicin	Gentocin	3	5 days	21 days
Penicillin G	injectable	1	5 days	5 days

Ampicillin. Many rabbits have died after several days' treatment with Amoxicillin (the manufacturers are the first to tell you not to use it in rabbits). Rarely have we used even injectable penicillin, and it has been along with gentamicin, for a more balanced spectrum, and at least 15cc per day of Lactobacillus acidophilus (oral liquid).

ANTIBIOTICS AND ANTIBODIES

Antibiotics function as either a bacteriostatic, which stops the growth of multiplying bacteria, or as a bactericidal, which stops metabolism within the bacterial cell and kills it. Both are used for rabbits.

The goal in antibiotic treatment is to buy time until the immune system can take over the job of destroying the infection. In rabbits this can take several weeks.

PROLONGED OR PERMANENT

As volunteers for the House Rabbit Society, we have rescued a large number of rabbits who are terminally or chronically ill, but with proper care, they lead fairly normal lives. And we can extend these lives by months and years.

Two major concerns with prolonged treatment are side effects (which we've rarely encountered with the drugs on our list) and bacterial resistance, a situation in which the bacteria we are trying to destroy become resistant to the antibiotic.

There is no fixed time, however, for this to occur and especially not in rabbits. In our experience, resistance has not developed quickly in rabbits, but antibiotics have a tough job because rabbits tend to wall off infections

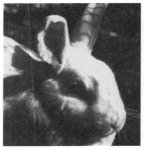

Long-term survivors. Left: Buzzie has been treated for a heart abscess for 14 months. Right: Sieglinda has been treated for an eye abscess for 2 years. Both have tetracycline (capsule form) in their drinking water.

into areas that the antibiotic can't reach. Antibiotics vary in their ability to penetrate inflammatory tissue and pus. Most don't do very well, but they do help check any bacteria that may leak out of a walled-off abscess and thus prevent spread to the rest of the body.

We are living with two such examples. Both rabbits have large, inaccessible abscesses—one near the heart; the other, behind the eye—which are simply held in check by tetracycline in the drinking water. One has been treated for over a year; the other, two years.

One of my greatest objections to traditional rabbit medicine is that veterinarians and rabbit owners have given up too soon, without realizing that even when there's not a complete cure, rabbits, in their own style, can be very resilient.

PHOTOS: BOB HARRIMAN

RISK-CUTTING SURGERY

WHEN SURGERY IS REQUIRED to remove an infection, a tumor, a hairball or a bladder stone, you have no choice but to proceed in order to improve your bunny's chance for survival. On the other hand, spaying or neutering is considered elective surgery, primarily intended to improve behavior and insure good toilet habits, in addition to preventing pregnancies. There are also health benefits, such as fewer infections due to bites and scratches and less inclination to urinary infections. And spayed females will never run the risk of uterine cancer (up to 80% in 5-year-olds).

In recent years, the House Rabbit Society has had close to a thousand rabbits spayed or neutered. We lost only one, and this was due to pre-existing liver disease. Since that occurrence, we have screened for liver disease, and our mortality rate for routine elective surgery has dropped to zero.

PRECAUTIONS AND PREPARATIONS

Of course we go to experienced vets, who do the job quickly and get the rabbit up from the anesthesia as soon as possible. We never fast our rabbits before or after surgery (remember, rabbits don't vomit). We have learned that they make a much quicker recovery if they don't miss a meal.

The safest time for surgery is 4 months to 1 year. We don't always have this age choice, however, and have opted for elective surgery on many 5 and 6-year-olds.

If you're making this decision for the first time, here are a few general guidelines.

*Males can be neutered as soon as the testicles have descended. This can happen any time after 3½ months.

*Females should be 6-8 months, depending on size.

*Rabbits over one year old (and younger ones who have been using pine or cedar litter) should have a basic pre-operative blood panel that checks for anemia, elevated liver enzymes and kidney function. This can usually be done in your vet's office at a nominal cost.

*If the blood test is ok, you can be more relaxed. If not, you can postpone surgery.

*If you have an exceptionally high-strung, nervous rabbit, let your vet know so that the bunny can be well sedated with pre-anesthetic before gas is given (especially important when using halothane).

BRINGING BUNNY HOME

Get a clean, disinfected cage ready. Your bunny should be confined for a few days to prevent overdoing—2 days for males, about 5 or 6 for females. Remove the litterbox if there is an inclination to sleep in it (and contaminate the suture area). Mixed sexes should be separated for about 2 weeks, in case of stored sperm, also to allow incisions to heal before sexual activity. Yes, many neutered pairs continue to be sexually active.

Usually, no antibiotic is necessary, but even so, some acidophilus and hay are good to get the GI tract going again. Most bunnies are able to eat immediately, but some may be anorexic for a couple of days.

TREATABLES/PREVENTABLES

MANY RABBIT HEALTH PROBLEMS are small ones that grow into big ones that could have been prevented in the first place. Human intervention can prevent or control many of the following situations:

Heat stress. It's too hot even in your house. Bunny pants and has a wet nose.

Prevention: Your freezer should have milk cartons full of ice to lay next to your bunny on hot days. Misting the ears with cool water can bring the temperature down. A wet towel across one end of the cage or run, with plenty of air blowing through, can make an evapora-tive cooler. Some bunnies enjoy a (supervised) full-body dip in a wading pool or the family pool.

Bleeding toenails. Bunny's toenails are too long. They're getting caught in carpeting or cage wire. They break and bleed, sometimes causing infection that may get into the bony tissue and necessitate eventual amputation.

Prevention: Keep toenails clipped—the colorless part—and have Kwik Stop on hand.

Malocclusion. The front teeth don't line up. They overgrow. Bunny can't eat.

Treatment: Clip teeth. It's easy with sharp

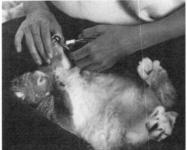

Wading pool (above). Eye drops (below)   *Toenail clip (above). Ear check (below)*   *Teeth clip (above). Flea powder (below).*

guillotine type (Resco) clippers. Have your vet show you. You can clip them nice and short without hurting bunny.

Conjunctivitis. Bunny's eyes are runny. There's no fever, and your vet has checked for abnormal eyelid structure and infection. Culture is negative.

Treatment: For some reason antibiotic eye medications often work. If allergens are suspected, a steroid-antibiotic combination might be prescribed.

Ear mites. You notice that the inside of bunny's ears are full of scabby material.

Treatment: Apply mineral oil or a local medication (one with a topical anesthetic for severe painful cases). The easiest way to get rid of mites of any kind—ear, skin and fur—is with the systemic treatment, Ivermectin, from your vet. Also used for heartworm in dogs, Ivermectin can be given orally or by injection. One dose, followed by a second a week later, will usually eliminate mites. Recheck often. They may still be in the environment.

Fleas/flea allergies. Your bunny is scratching a lot and losing hair. You may or may not see the fleas, but you see other evidence (grainy flea manure). Very severe infestations can be the direct cause of anemia.

Treatment: Cat flea powders can be used on rabbits. We have used them for years with no adverse effects. Also, you can treat your rugs every 6 months with non-aerosol spray from your pet supply store. You can spray one room at a time, with the bunnies in another room or outside for a few hours.

Fur mites (cheyletiella). To the casual observer these are indistinguishable from flea allergies—bald spots and scaly skin.

Treatment: a combination of flea powder externally; Ivermectin orally.

Sore hocks (foot sores). Bunny sits all the time in the litterbox. Finally, you turn her over and notice red bald spots, maybe some pus, on the bottoms of her feet. Sitting in urine has compounded the problem.

Prevention: Some rabbits are better equipped with natural padding, but if nature doesn't supply it, you can—with rugs. Very simply, the bony area on the feet cannot come into contact with hard or abrasive surfaces (e.g. wooden floors, cage wire).

A washable rug (described on page 83) can keep bunny's feet padded while in the cage. If her feet have open sores, clean them with Xenodine 2-3 times daily.

Urine burn. Due to other conditions bunny can't "posture" properly to urinate. Urine-soaked fur causes inflammation.

Treatment: Apply Panalog ointment to inflamed flesh daily. Vaseline can be used as protection after inflammation has cleared.

Fly strike. A life-threatening complication to other problems. A bunny with oozy sores or wet rear-end should be kept strictly indoors.

Ingested synthetics. Bunny has gobbled down the rubber band from your newspaper, or he may have grazed on your shag carpet.

Treatment: Assume there's potential for intestinal blockage. Dose for a few days with petroleum laxative.

SPECIAL NEEDS OF THE VERY YOUNG

WHENEVER I RECEIVE a frantic phone call from rabbit owners of "accidental" offspring, I always give a lecture on the necessity of spaying and neutering before giving advice on taking care of the babies.

Now, let's assume the accident has already taken place. A young adolescent mother in a bewildered state has dropped a bunch of babies behind your kitchen door. You're unprepared, and the stores are closed.

WHAT TO DO

1. Get some kind of box—about 12"x14". The sides can be about 8" high, but the front should be no higher than 4" where Mama Bunny steps over it.

2. Put in a 3-inch layer of clean yellow straw or finely shredded paper (wood shavings can be used temporarily, without causing permanent liver damage).

3. Make a "well" in the middle of the nestbox with your fist and fill with fur from the mother. If she hasn't pulled enough out herself, clip some.

4. Put the babies in this "well of fur" (yes, you can handle them). They will burrow to the bottom and stay there until nursing time.

5. Show Mother Bunny where her babies are but don't expect her to get in there with them. Other than an occasional investigation of the nest box, she won't attend them until nursing time, which probably won't be until long after you're in bed.

Rabbits nurse only once a day. Rabbit milk is very rich and can sustain the babies for 24 hours. The babies remain under the fur until Mother stands over them to nurse. If you really don't think she is nursing, you can find out for sure by weighing the babies daily (I use a postage scale). If they are gaining weight, she is feeding them.

THE ORPHANED LITTER

Hand raising is very difficult. Yet we have rescued hundreds of orphan bunnies from animal shelters and raised them successfully by these steps:

1. Set up nestbox as described earlier.

2. Obtain fur from any healthy rabbit.

3. Provide warmth. Several babies brood each other (share body heat), but one or two need help. I keep the room temperature at 70° night and day. I don't trust heating pads, but one can be attached to the side of an open nestbox (monitor closely).

4. Wash faces and bottoms with warm water and cotton after each meal, for cleanliness and to help with elimination.

HAND FEEDING

Hand feeding is very tricky. You can bottle feed, syringe feed or tube feed. Bottle feeding requires a perfect nipple. I use only Pet-Ag (formerly Borden's) nursing bottles and snip off the thickness of rubber at the end of the nipple so that I'm punching a hole through thinner rubber. The hole should allow a fine spray. When testing on your arm the milk should not come out in large drops, nor should you have to shake the bottle vigorously to get a few tiny drops. Once you get a perfect nipple, bottle feeding is easy and can be done just twice a day.

"Once you get a perfect nipple, bottle feeding is easy..."

Syringes can be used, but this technique is messier because much of the formula dribbles down the chin and neck. The babies lap up the formula from the end of the syringe rather than draw with suction from a rubber nipple. Once you start them with syringes you can't switch to a bottle because they lose their nursing reflex very quickly (within 2 days). Syringe feedings are more frequent (5-6 times a day) because less is consumed at a time.

Enjoying a meal: this rescued orphan, shown here at 9-days-old, was completely hand raised (and later adopted) along with her brother.

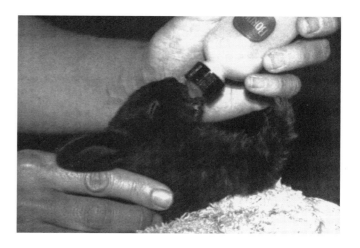

The danger with hand feeding is that the liquid can get into the air passage and the baby strangles or develops pneumonia. My own preference for nursing bottles is because the baby's natural sucking motion closes the larynx and minimizes the possibility of aspiration.

The windpipe can be bypassed entirely, by inserting a feeding tube directly into the stomach. This procedure is obviously not for a novice and should be done by your veterinarian, or have your vet instruct you.

WHAT TO FEED

Canned KMR (kitten formula) from the pet supply store and Lactobacillus acidophilus from the health food store make a suitable bunny formula (In rural areas goat milk is often used).

Bunnies can nibble on dry alfalfa and a few pellets as they show interest—at 2-3 weeks. The increase in formula consumption levels off at about 4 weeks, but don't rush weaning.

ORPHAN FORMULA-FEEDING PROGRAM
Whether you do it in two feedings or several, this is the approximate *daily* quantitiy. Increase gradually.

Table 2. Formula requirements per age

AGE	KMR	ACIDOPHILUS
Newborn	5 cc	½ cc
1 week old	12-15 cc	1 cc
2 weeks old	25-27cc	1 cc
3 weeks old	30 cc	2 cc
4 weeks old	30 cc	2 cc

Babies need lactic acid from their mother or from the acidophilus to help get good intestinal flora started. This is more important, not less important, as they begin to eat solid food. Nursing until 6 or 7 weeks helps reduce risk of fatal diarrhea. I recommend acidophilus in the drinking water until 12 weeks.

After the 12th week a small carrot chunk can be offered but hold off on greens, fruit, and cracker treats until about 16 weeks.

HOME NURSING CARE

Octavia, our nursemaid cat, washes her ailing friend. We never knew if it was the Ditrim injections or the daily cat-assisted therapy that pulled Phoebe through her bout with pneumonia.

IF YOUR BUNNY IS RECOVERING from a serious illness, there may be support that can be continued at home. Depending on the disease, there are several things useful to learn.

Injections—even if you're squeamish about needles, rabbits, unlike many cats, make it easy for you. Most of their injections can be given subcutaneously (under the skin) between the shoulders, and they seldom even wince over a shot given there.

Also, a convalescing rabbit often needs subcutaneous fluids. This is not only to keep up hydration but it balances the electrolytes and also helps flush out toxins. Lactated Ringer's Solution (LRS) is given for a number of conditions including: toxicity, kidney malfunction, fever, and constipation.

The LRS bag is set up in such a way that B-vitamins can be added, which is often a good thing to do for an ailing anorexic rabbit. Your vet will give you lessons if this treatment is prescribed. You don't need special hospital equipment. I simply hook the bag onto a coat hanger and hang it on a camera tripod.

WHAT ABOUT INVALIDS?

Millions of humans are on lifelong medication, for everything from allergies to heart disease, and no one questions their quality of life. We don't destroy humans who are missing a limb or have a physical impairment. Many kinds of infirmity do not involve pain, so let's be careful about judging from appearances alone. If you have learned your rabbit's body language, you can sense a will to live.

Does he enjoy his meals? Does he enjoy being petted? Does he turn his ears towards intriguing sounds? Are his eyes bright? Does he show an interest when the cat walks by and in the things going on around him?

House Rabbit Society volunteers have lived with many invalid rabbits. Often our paraplegics and quadriplegics are wonderful animals. Don't be so appalled by outward defor-

PHOTO: MARINELL HARRIMAN

mity. Inside may be a cheerful and well-adjusted bunny. If you have such an animal, there are ways to minimize your work. A disabled rabbit can no longer hop into the litterbox, so other arrangements have to be made. Depending on the degree of immobility, two options are available: Pampers (newborn size) are marvelous for an incontinent rabbit. Just as with human children, they draw the moisture away from the tender flesh. We had a rabbit in Pampers for nearly a year, and she never once suffered from urine burn. She could scoot around on the floor freely, and there were no soiled rugs.

CUSHIONED COMFORT

A completely immobile rabbit can be kept on a special rug from the pet supply store. These are washable synthetic-sheepskin rugs that, like Pampers, draw the moisture away from the flesh. Rugs without a rubber backing are preferable because you don't want to trap the moisture inside the rug (next to your rabbit). If bunny's rug is on the floor, simply put newspapers underneath it.

In situations where urine burn does occur, a generous application of Panalog (ointment or cream) is a good cure. It does a great job on inflamed flesh and also dissolves caked-on feces. A very sick rabbit should not be given a full-body bath (except to bring down a fever), so "spot washing" with running water is safer.

FEEDING TECHNIQUES

Some disabled rabbits are able to feed themselves. Most can drink more easily from a water bottle than from a bowl. If the bunny's digestion is greatly impaired, or if chewing is a problem, hand feeding may be necessary, at least part of the time. It's not difficult, once you get the strategy worked out. The following formula was devised to be consumed by a 6-pound rabbit within a 24-hour period. Measurements should be adjusted to size.

- Soak ½ cup dry pellets in 1 cup water.
- Run through blender at medium speed for 5-10 minutes. (This is the right consistency for a feeding syringe.)
- After the mixture is blended, stir in ¼ teaspoon Prozyme or Nutrazyme to further aid digestion.

The amount that can be fed at 4-5 hour intervals is about 50 cc (for a 6 lb. rabbit). Your vet can provide you with large feeding-syringes.

If your job schedule prevents such regular feedings, you will have to leave easily accessible foods, such as vegetables and hay, for your bun to feed himself in your absence. These are better left loose on his rug as he may have trouble reaching into his bowl.

A JOB WELL DONE

Your last responsibility to your invalid is to provide entertainment. Remember how he has entertained you all of his life. Talk to him. Pet him. Move him around to different locations so that he doesn't get bored. Spend quality time. These are precious moments, and someday you will be grateful that you had this time.

About Friendship

CHAPTER

5

OFTEN, SINGLE-RABBIT owners are so gratified by their first experience that they want to repeat it. This is a good reason to consider adopting a second rabbit. Another is that rabbits are sociable animals, whose lives are happiest when shared with at least one additional

Display of tenderness: House rabbit Nibble (Opposite) gladly accepts it from guinea pig Hank. House rabbit Lillian (right) receives her love from house rabbit Cecil.

friend. This can be yourself, a second rabbit, or another household animal.

If your own time at home has decreased and you feel that your bunny is lonely, you can still provide companionship. Think about a pet for your pet.

House Rabbit Society volunteers usually have not only multiple rabbits but also multiple species. We have been forced to find answers to compatibility problems because space limitations make it difficult to house them separately. Neutering has been a necessity. It allows social activity that could not otherwise exist. We have been able to observe group behavior and draw conclusions helpful in introducing animals to each other. This chapter will explore some of the options.

PHOTOS: MARINELL HARRIMAN

RABBIT TO RABBIT FRIENDSHIP

A cautious meeting: Sophie (inside the box) waits with apprehension while Susie checks her out.

Rabbits don't always know that their matches were made in heaven. Actually, a group is easier to put together than two individuals at a time. This may be due to a natural tendency of rabbits to fall into a hierarchical structure. On the other hand we've found that some rabbits are much more monogamous than others and living as bonded pairs is more natural for them.

The easiest introduction is between a neutered male and a spayed female. Friendship between two females is more likely than between two males (neutered, of course).

Neutering does not end all sexual activity, so don't accuse your vet of blundered surgery when you see your rabbits spin themselves into a passionate courtship. We who observe this phenomenon conclude that rabbit sexuality is largely a mental attitude.

Always make the introduction in neutral territory that is not part of either rabbit's normal environment. The territory should be large enough to allow a little distance between them, but not so large that they forget the existence of the other rabbit. A single room, a porch or a backyard playpen is ideal (not much larger than 10 x 12, or smaller than 3 x 8). Sometimes a ride in the car to a friend's house will help prepare them for a new situation. The aim here is to eliminate any territorial possessiveness. Here are possible scenarios:

Plan A—*when a new couple takes to each other immediately and remains inseparable for the rest of their lives.* This does happen occasionally. When this instant magic occurs, they don't need supervision or limited exposure or any intervention on your part. All you will need are whiskbroom and dustpan, sponge and white vinegar. Temporarily, you will have some extra cleanup. In their excitement most "honeymooners" forsake their good toilet habits for a couple of days.

Plan B—*when the intended couple show interest with reservation.* This is more common. They do not fall in love at first sight, but there's not yet any real antagonism. So far, so good. Take it slow and easy. Keep them separated except for a 20 minute period once a day in the neutral territory.

Supervise the first few days. There may be some chasing and nipping, but if there's no fur flying or flesh being ripped, let them work

PHOTO: MARINELL HARRIMAN

things out for themselves. If no real fighting has occurred for several consecutive days, you can increase their time together to an hour or more. You can also discontinue supervision except to check on them from time to time.

You will notice them sitting on opposite sides of the territory. Gradually you will see them sitting closer together. It may take several weeks, but you will finally see them snuggling together during the day. Give them a few more days to firmly establish this cordial habit, then they are ready to share a bed and can remain together at night.

Plan C—*when the intended couple take an instant dislike to each other and engage in an immediate fight.* Things don't look too promising, but if you're determined to make them buddies, you will have to put forth extra effort. Start with Plan B but limit exposure to shorter, more frequent sessions and protect yourself with gloves and jacket while breaking up fights. Another way (not to be used in cold weather) is to preside over them with a water pistol. A third technique is to have both on harness and leash and pull them apart before they have a chance to chomp down. Add to the above steps persistence.

A note of caution for health reasons. As much as we encourage companionship for all rabbits, a new introduction is a stressful period. Whether it's happy excitement or not, it puts an extra load on the immune system. If you're working with an older animal or one in delicate health, proceed slowly. If your bunny is prone to snuffles or diarrhea, use Plan B

instead of Plan A and proceed slowly no matter how ecstatic he is over his new playmate. Limit the exposure to short daily periods and gradually increase the time.

Twice the charm: This pair of Milwaukee sisters will tell you how worthwhile it is to have two bunnies.

THE NATURALLY SOCIABLE

Some insight on rabbit social behavior comes from a rabbit foster home in Placerville, California, where Margo DeMello and her husband, Shannon Shirley, have a unique living arrangement with a "warren" of 25 rabbits. Their rabbits are neutered and can interact freely with each other. They have access to a communal play yard (via a pet door) by day but are secured in the house at night. They find their own cages indoors where they settle down in pairs or groups for the night.

The behavior observed in the DeMello warren is of greater value to the pet owner than a

Triple charm: Dinah and Dominique are happy to share snuggles with Lefty, their male companion.

study of wild rabbits. Margo's observations may answer some of your questions:

1. Rabbits tend to be possessive with their cages. Obviously, when the purpose is not to hold prisoners, cages can be quite desirable as resting and feeding places.

2. Big open spaces are regarded as neutral.

3. Rabbits who are interested in "social climbing" tend to acquire multiple mates.

4. Rabbits who are monogamous are less interested in the group power struggle.

5. Presenting (dropping the head forward) is a submissive gesture used by rabbits who are approached by more dominant rabbits. Submission is not necessarily unpleasant—as when your rabbit presents while being petted.

6. Presenting is also a gesture used by dominant rabbits who expect to be groomed by subordinates. If your rabbit charges at you and then presents, you probably have a king or a queen who expects you to do your duty and start petting.

Group Behavior

By Margo DeMello

UNLIKE MANY ANIMALS *whose social system is based on kinship. rabbits' social life is focused on a system of dominance. In my group of 25 rabbits who share a room and a yard, the individual relationships are striking. We have one king, and two queens. Dominance is based on four main factors: age, size, personality, and position in a "family" group. Those rabbits who cannot attract a number of mates, male or female, will not gain a very high status, no matter how big or outgoing they may be.*

We also have princes and princesses, less dominant bunnies who are struggling to better their positions. Finally there are the subordinate rabbits.

Those who live or socialize with dominant rabbits are protected and happy. Those who don't must constantly fight to protect their position, or must always submit to the more dominant, by either "presenting" when he or she nears, or just by getting out of the way. The dominant rabbits get groomed by the subordinates; they also get the first choice at food and the best spots to rest. Actual fighting rarely occurs, usually just when someone's cage is invaded, when someone is snuggling with another rabbit's mate, or when a subordinate rabbit or a newcomer challenges a dominant rabbit's authority. ☙

PHOTO: BOB HARRIMAN

RABBITS WITH CATS

ALTHOUGH RABBITS ARE SOCIABLE, the demands of their own society can be too stressful for some individuals to live happily. These animals often relate better to companions of another species.

Cats and rabbits in the same household can develop some interesting relationships. Not all have the same rapport as my Phoebe and Octavia, but many can find fun in other ways.

Our first rabbit, Herman, and our cat, Nice, never touched, but they interacted in chase games—in and out of paper bags. Phoebe, Herman's successor, intimidates Nice (on page 13) and adores Octavia (on this page). Friendship is determined by individuals.

Introductions during feisty adolescence of either species should be more carefully supervised. A lively, boisterous teenage cat can put dangerous claws into an unsuspecting bunny. And, of course, you should avoid giving a very young bunny (rat size) to a full-grown cat. On the other hand, big rabbits can bully a lighter weight cat, so equal size usually makes a better match.

Through thick and thin: It's Phoebe's turn to groom Octavia, the cat who takes care of ailing rabbits (page 82).

PHOTO: MARINELL HARRIMAN

RABBITS WITH DOGS

FROM THE DAY I CAME HOME from work to find my then 14-year-old son, Bill, with his dog, Rags, and our rabbit, Herman, sitting on the bedroom floor doing "homework," I never gave much thought to dogs and rabbits in the same house. Of course our dog is extremely amenable. She literally lets the guinea pigs walk all over her, and she had been through basic obedience training, which I took for granted.

Successful rabbit-dog introductions are largely dependent on the behavior of the dog, and it's absolutely crucial that the dog not chase if the rabbit runs. Since dog behavior is the key factor here, a mature, easy-going, obedience-trained dog is generally the best candidate for companionship with a rabbit. He should know "down-stay," "gentle," "good dog," and "off" before an introduction is attempted.

My friend Amy Shapiro teaches dog-training classes at a humane society and keeps rabbits, cats and dogs in her home. For the initial introduction Amy advises, "If the rabbit is skittish and/or the dog is rambunctious, have the rabbit in her cage and the dog on-leash." Amy's article "When Fido Met Thumper" is available through the House Rabbit Society.

PHOTO: AMY SHAPIRO

RABBITS WITH SMALLER FRIENDS

INTERACTION WITH SMALLER ANIMALS, such as hamsters, mice and sometimes birds, will vary with the individuals, but any additional interest in the environment is better than loneliness and boredom.

Guinea pigs can be compatible with rabbits. Some people enjoy building them elaborate habitats as they do for their rabbits. Sometimes a fenced-in playground is provided that the pigs and bunnies can share. The fence or wall can be as low as 1 foot high if you want your rabbits, but not your guinea pigs, to have access to the rest of the house.

We let our guinea pigs have part-time run of the house. They are hilarious to watch as they propel their massive little bodies around on ridiculously small feet (when you're used to looking at rabbits). Their litterbox needs are different—many little flat trays along the edges of the room and under beds.

They will eat rabbit pellets but have additional vitamin C requirements. Their antibiotic sensitivities are similar, but guinea pigs have very specific physical needs. If this is your companion of choice for your rabbit, please get a good book on guinea pig care.

They seem to fall into fairly easy friendships with rabbits and have a lot to offer.

Natural friends

By Elizabeth TeSelle

"HOW CAN YOU LET your rabbits run around the house with your cats?" people always ask me. "Aren't they natural enemies?" When they hear we also have two dogs, they stare in disbelief.

I just smile, thinking of our peaceable kingdom, consisting of three cats, two dogs and three rabbits. Introducing the three species to each other was far less complicated than introducing members of the same species. While Melissa, the mini-lop, refuses to get along with Charlie, the Angora, she and my cat Loki often share the same resting place under the couch.

As for the dogs, Greta and Ellie were gracious and friendly from the start. Obedience trained, they are accustomed to looking to us for guidance and learned quickly that inquisitive sniffing is acceptable, while rough play is not.

Our resident lapines are free-running Jeremy and Melissa, and young Charlie, who is supervised when free. Because Charlie is energetic, I was concerned that his gymnastic feats would excite the dogs, but they seem to understand his fragility. When Charlie comes barrelling across the living room and skids between their legs, Greta and Ellie freeze in place until he has cleared them.

Far from being natural enemies, our rabbits, cats, and dogs have become the best of natural friends. Animals, after all, are not stupid. Greta and Ellie would not hesitate to chase a wild rabbit if given the opportunity, and before she met me, my cat Ebony killed for a living, but they all seem to understand readily that Jeremy, Melissa and Charlie are in a different class altogether.

By far the most rewarding part of living in a multiple-species household is watching the animals learn to communicate with each other despite their genetic differences. Getting to know another species adds richness and depth to anyone's life. Certainly my companion animals are better off for having known one another, just as I am better off for having shared my life with all of them. ☙

RABBITS WITH PEOPLE

Perfection in all: Susan Stark loves every bunny, a houseful of fosters and her own pampered pair, Nikita and Barney.

WHATEVER ADDITIONAL companions you have chosen to introduce to your bunny one of them will be yourself. Rabbit to human introductions are sometimes complicated because you both are learning a new language, and there may be a few misinterpretations along the way.

Like many worthwhile goals, a perfect relationship requires an investment of time and effort. As we work our way through a few of the possible problems, we can identify, understand, and minimize them.

NIPS, TUCKS, AND BITES

Testing: It's common for baby rabbits to go through a period of testing their teeth. If your bunny decides to test his teeth on you, I advise a small screech. This is a sound rabbits make in dire distress. He will understand that this is serious business.

Move-over: Rabbits may nip what's in their way. It can be another rabbit who is blocking the water bottle or a human arm that is confining a rabbit to a lap. Screeching may work, but it might be better to avoid using part of your body as a barricade.

Overly-zealous: When grooming each other, rabbits pull out burrs and chew foreign particles entangled in each other's fur. Keep this in mind when your rabbit friend is licking your sleeve or pant leg and comes to a seam or wrinkle that could be interpreted as "foreign."

Defensive biting: Sometimes objects coming from below eye level may appear threatening. Don't stick your hand up to a rabbit's nose to be sniffed as you would to a dog or scratch him under the chin like a cat. Pet from the top. Also, it's considerably more difficult to approach an apprehensive rabbit from a side opening cage.

WHERE'S THE CUDDLY BUNNY?

Your rabbit may not instinctively want to sit entrapped on your lap. To persuade him that this is a pleasant place, it's best to reach him at his level, which is on the floor. We tell this to children often. Sit on the floor and read a book or watch TV, and the bunny will come to you. He can't help it. His natural curiosity will bring him to you. He will nudge and sniff you and hop onto your lap. Let him hop on and off at will. A towel spread across your lap will make it more inviting to your bunny, and you will be glad it's between you and the toenails

"Two positions that I use are shoulder-rump and feet-to-chest."

that are trying to get a foothold.

Rabbits groom each other around the eyes, top of the nose, top of the head, ears, and down the back. Stroking them in these areas is readily understood as friendly. They also understand face-to-face intimacy.

FRIENDLY LIFTING

Rabbits enjoy cozying up beside you, but being lifted and carried is a different matter. There are times when it can't be avoided. For this reason I recommend a daily exercise in lifting and handling by just picking her up and setting her down again. A brief, non-stressful lift followed by a small reward will help a rabbit overcome the fear of being lifted. Our formerly reluctant Phoebe caught on quickly. She soon began to circle my feet, tripping me, if I forgot her cracker when I set her down.

Our foster rabbits must be carried daily to their exercise-pens, and trial-and-error has provided lifting techniques that work for most.

Two positions that I use are shoulder-rump and feet-to-chest. I lift all larger rabbits by the shoulders and rump. This is best done from behind. If they're facing toward me, I turn them around. Any that tend to kick are held with the hindquarters firm and low. I don't want their hind feet in kicking position. As anticipation gets the better of them, they are more inclined to kick as they are being set down. If you feel your bunny kicking right out of your arms, drop into an immediate squat on the floor. Reducing the height will reduce the chances of injury to your bunny or yourself.

Smaller rabbits tend to feel more secure with their front feet resting on your collar bone. I usually scoop them toward me into this position. Whatever style you develop in picking up your own rabbit will seem the only right way to her.

PHOTO LEFT: BOB HARRIMAN. RIGHT: AMY SHAPIRO

"...you will be brought to the floor like everyone else."

WHAT YOU CAN BUILD

Whatever material you have to work with—a quiet, docile, nosy, assertive, or independent bunny *and* a caring human—you will have all that you need to create a beautiful friendship. Besides the joy of communication with a true companion, you will also derive pleasure from watching her response to the things you provide—toys, treats, comforts.

So what, if the rug needs mending? It's a small price to pay for your therapist and her soothing ointment on your wounds of the day. If your stresses do not not disappear, they will at least diminish in size.

Those of us whose rabbits occupy our hearts and homes know the power of these quiet creatures. They have brought us not only down to our knees but prostrate to the floor. Yes, you'll wind up there too. However high your social standing or economic worth, you will be brought to the floor like everyone else who lives with a house rabbit. But from this lower vantage point you may finally see things accurately. You will have to restructure your priorities when your house rabbit points out to you that you have been placing value on the wrong things. After all, what can be more important than petting a rabbit?

PHOTO: MARINELL HARRIMAN

ENDNOTES

Chapter 1. The intrepetation of rabbit language is a consensus drawn from the daily observations of volunteers in California who have rescued and lived with over 1,100 rabbits.

Chapter 2. Sources cited in text

Chapter 3. Volunteers and individual rabbit owners across the country who have supplied practical information on living with a rabbit: Amy Shapiro, Helen Lau, Franklin Chow, Susan Stark, Betty Tsubamoto, Lynda Alston, Bill Webb, Judy Morin, Terry and Jesus Valerio, Carolyn Long, Sylvia Johnson, Jim Johnson, Dena Sharp, Melanie Cresci, Kim Stiewig, Tamara Leaf Sortman, Robin Sortman, Victoria Marney-Petix, Diana Murphy, Mark Lichtenfeld, Bill Yaden. Elizabeth TeSelle, Barbara Pollack, Sandi Ackerman, Kari S. Gilje, and Kay Leiker, and Laura George.

The Poison chart is compiled from information obtained from the following poison centers: Texas State Poison Center, The University of Texas, Galveston, TX; Hennepin Poison Center, Minneapolis, MN; St. Mary's Regional Medical Center, Reno, NV; Oregon Poison Center, Portland, OR; NYC Poison Control Center, New York, NY; San Francisco Bay Area Regional Poison Control Center, San Francisco, CA; University of California Irvine Medical Center, Orange, CA; Arizona Poison Control, Tucson, AZ; The Illinois Animal Poison Information Center, Urbana, IL; The Intermountain Regional Poison Control Center, Salt Lake City, UT; Regional Poison Center, Jacksonville, FL.

Chapter 4. Sources are Marliss Geissler, DVM, Carolynn Harvey, DVM and Richard Evans, DVM, MS. Drs. Geissler and Harvey have extensive hands-on experience with rabbits from practicing in a hospital that schedules over 2,000 rabbit office visits a year.

Dr. Evans, now director of the Pacific Wildlife Project, a non-profit rehabilitation center in Southern California, formerly headed the diagnostic lab for rabbits at Ralston Purina in St. Louis. His findings, from his work there, have been published in scientific journals.

Also, my son, Bill Harriman, who is working on his Ph D. in immunology, has supplied general health information from UC San Francisco

Chapter 5. Results of experiments with group living in foster homes come from Amy Shapiro, Susan Stark, Margo DeMello, Holly O'Meara, and Helen Lau.

Multi-species information sources are Elizabeth TeSelle, a volunteer at the Bloomington Animal Shelter in Bloomington, Indiana and Amy Shapiro, animal behaviorist and dog trainer at the Peninsula Humane Society in San Mateo, California.

INDEX